THE POWER OF BELIEVING

J. Ellsworth Kalas

THE POWER OF BELIEVING

WORD BOOKS
PUBLISHER
WACO, TEXAS
A DIVISION OF
WORD, INCORPORATED

THE POWER OF BELIEVING

Copyright © 1987 by J. Ellsworth Kalas

All rights reserved. No portion of this book may be reproduced in any form without the written permission of the publishers, except for brief quotations in book reviews, etc. Unless otherwise indicated, Scripture quotations are from the Revised Standard Version of the Bible, copyrighted 1946, 1952, © 1971, 1973 by the Division of Christian Education of the National Council of Churches of Christ in the U.S.A. Used by permission. Those marked KJV are from the authorized King James Version. Those marked NIV are from the New International Version of the Bible, copyright © 1978 by the International Bible Society.

Library of Congress Cataloging in Publication Data

Kalas, J. Ellsworth, 1923–
   The power of believing.

   1. Faith.   2. Christian life—Methodist authors.
I. Title.
BV4637.K35   1987   234'.2   87-14076
ISBN 0-8499-0568-0

Printed in the United States of America

7 8 9 8 RRD 9 8 7 6 5 4 3 2 1

To
TADDY
*who walks with laughter
and shares it extravagantly*

Contents

Introduction 9
1. Faith Is a Laughing Matter 13
2. Faith Comes with Our Original Equipment 33
3. Why Is Faith So Important? 51
4. The Faith That Holds On 67
5. Faith That Moves Mountains 89
6. If You See It You Can Have It! 107
Study Guide 127

Introduction

Faith, like the weather, is a subject everybody talks about but few do anything about. Part of the problem is that so many who talk about faith don't even realize that they're doing so. They think of faith as a mystical quality possessed by a few rare souls. As a result, they have no idea of the potential for faith in their own lives.

I have tried through this book to bring faith more nearly within reach. It is not a scarce commodity meted out stingily by an unfriendly God; it is as near and constant as the air we breathe, and it expresses itself in the sound of good laughter.

I think I have opened some new insights in this book. I have tried to do so in the simplest fashion possible, for if faith comes by hearing, it's essential that I make these ideas as "hearable" as possible. The insights have come to me through literally hundreds of channels, but primarily through the Scriptures. I am indebted to so many people, yet I can't trace many of the ideas to specific individuals. Rather, they are pieces that have come together in significant fashion in my own life.

I am very specifically indebted, however, as far as the development of this book is concerned. At the time I began preparing it for Word Books, I had not yet written a book.

Introduction

Many kind persons had encouraged me to do so over the years, but the Rev. Susan Sharpe, who was then on our church staff, not only encouraged me, she insisted. Then, on her own, she sent some of my ideas and sermons to "Frog" Sullivan, who in turn passed them along to some of his friends at Word, until I found myself at last in the care of Floyd Thatcher, who nurtured my work through its many weaknesses to a more acceptable form; and more recently, Al Bryant. Both men have a gift for friendship. In the rather hectic world of publishing, they are Christian gentlemen.

I am also indebted to Margaret Speed, who has typed this manuscript. Retired from a secretarial career, she has given her skills generously. "Do you have another chapter ready for me?" became her standard greeting on Sunday mornings.

One can't survive in this world without a minimum supply of faith; and the larger the supply and the better we apply it, the more gladly and victoriously we can live. I pray that God, in His goodness, will use this book to that end in the lives of those who read it.

J. ELLSWORTH KALAS

When we laugh, we are expressing the conviction that something is still right with the world, or if it isn't right at the moment, it will be some day. It is true, of course, that certain kinds of laughter are sometimes badly perverted. Tragically, none of God's gifts—from sex to healing drugs—has been free from perversion and abuse. But when laughter is used the way God intended it to be, we can know that God is enjoying it too.

{ 1 }

Faith Is a Laughing Matter

THERE WASN'T MUCH LAUGHTER IN JANIS the first time we met more than twenty years ago. She was a patient in the psychiatric unit of St. Mary's Hospital in Madison, Wisconsin. When Janis had been admitted, she listed our church as her religious affiliation even though she had only attended a few times.

Her face was as plain and dull as her hospital garb. I could see that she was drained and defeated. And while she was courteous enough to acknowledge my presence, she responded to my attempts at friendliness in as few syllables as possible.

Janis had good reason to be depressed. Life had dealt her a pretty mean hand. She was born with mild hydrocephalus, plus spina bifida. When she was 21, the spinal growth was removed, but other deeper and more lasting ills had developed. Because of her physical limitations, including brain spasms which caused seizures much like epileptic attacks, she felt like a social outcast. And to compound her emotional injuries, Janis had learned, even as a small child, that she was a disappointment to her father. Then when a beautiful and normal baby sister had been born into the family a few years later, her sense of unworthiness became even more intense.

I learned that Janis had grown up in the church and had found acceptance there, especially in the youth activities. But the church had also complicated her problems in an ironic way. She identified herself with the Beatitudes because she found personal consolation in the feeling that they applied especially to her: she understood those who suffer, mourn, and are persecuted—these words described her way of life.

No one ever told Janis that the word "blessed" in those beatitudes is better translated "happy." Janis knew what it was to feel hurt and sad and shut out. For her, being blessed seemed to be found in being miserable. Unfortunately, many Christians seem at times to share the feeling Janis had that the best evidence of the good life is to be found in pain.

After taking training to be a licensed practical nurse, Janis found work in Madison, some forty miles from her hometown. But the years of seizures had caused some brain deterioration, and her low self-esteem only added to her inability to respond in a wholesome way to life's daily problems.

"I felt like I had the weight of the whole world on my shoulders, and I couldn't cope any more," she now recalls. It was at this time that she was admitted—utterly despondent and defeated—to the psychiatric ward.

After several weeks of hospitalization, Janis was released as an outpatient while she continued her treatment. But when she tried to return to her job, her supervisors had decided she was no longer employable. Thus she was given disability retirement. Janis was still in her early forties, and to her this seemed like the final humiliation.

But now that Janis had more time, she became involved in several church activities. "As I listened to your Sunday sermons," she said, "now and then I'd say to myself, 'Hey, he seems to think something better is going to happen some day.' But I'd spent so much of my life feeling guilty about my illnesses, for being a disappointment to my father, and for not being as attractive as my sister—crazy things like that—that I couldn't really hear what you were saying.

"Then it was in Mrs. Kalas's Bible studies that I first began to laugh. Some of the things she said about certain women in the Bible struck me as being very funny. I'd never thought of them that way before. Then I began to look at myself and laugh. I even felt a little bit guilty about the way I was feeling. But it felt good to laugh, and this was a whole new experience for me. Up to then I hadn't found much in my life to laugh about."

Laughter Lends Perspective

C. S. Lewis once said that the ability to laugh at oneself is functionally the closest thing to true repentance. After all, when we laugh, we see ourselves in perspective, but we also see ourselves through lenses of kindness and hope. This is what was happening to Janis.

She needed to know and really believe that she was a person of worth—that she was somebody. "I had to realize," she said, "that it was my body that had failed, and that I myself was still worth something."

Taking courage from her new feelings and the beginning of a new hope, Janis applied to become a foster parent. At that time, though, a single foster parent was unheard of, and, of course, her health record and future prospects were not encouraging. But she wouldn't take no for an answer. Thus she persisted until the authorities began to weaken.

One day I received an inquiry from a social worker associated with the State Division of Children and Youth. They had a baby with Downs syndrome who was profoundly retarded and had a bad heart. It was felt the child would only live a short time but he would be better off placed in a home. The social worker asked, "Do you believe Janis can handle the responsibility of such a baby?" Without a moment's hesitation I answered, "Absolutely. Her own experience with frustration and defeat will help her understand and empathize with this little baby in a special way. And if by any chance he should live, she can teach him to cope with his limitations."

Timmy was three weeks old when he came into Janis's home. From the very beginning she surrounded him with love and laughter. Her own life had been profoundly changed as she had seen what joy, laughter, and love had done for her. She had come to see that this God-given joy and laughter didn't depend on circumstances or humor. Rather, it springs from deep within the heart of faith. She had learned there is healing in laughter, and she wanted to see Timmy healed.

When Timmy celebrated his second birthday, the doctors labeled him a miracle. And now, as I write this story, he is nineteen years old and able to manage far more of life's complexities than the most optimistic doctors would have predicted. Janis tells it this way, "He's gone from profoundly retarded to severely retarded to moderately retarded. Now they score him as only mildly retarded."

To all of us in the church community who have loved Janis and Timmy and have stood by them over the years, Timmy is a continuing miracle. But in so many ways Janis is the greater miracle. There is nothing easy about her life. In addition to everything else, she now has a malignancy, and her finances are very limited. But she continues to handle life with joy and laughter.

Short and stocky, with a staccato speech pattern that insists on earnest attention, Janis might be expected to meet resistance in the typical upper middle class congregation.

But the transparent reality of her faith attracts people to her. She has a faith-joy that gets the attention of even the spiritually jaundiced. And those who don't know her story realize that she has experienced something real and are inspired by her exuberance.

A Woman's Worth

In so many ways Janis reminds me of Abraham's wife, Sarah, that magnificent Old Testament lady. All her life Sarah waited and hoped for a child, but the miracle of conception hadn't happened. She was a failure. A woman's worth in those days depended on her ability to bear children, and any woman who couldn't was considered out of favor with God.

But Sarah had been true to God. She had followed Abraham when he packed up the family belongings and left a city of culture to find a better place that wasn't even on the map—"A city with foundations whose builder and maker was God" (Heb. 11:10). Undoubtedly at that time Sarah was pretty well satisfied with life in Ur of the Chaldees, but she turned her back on everything familiar and comfortable and went with Abraham. And there is no hint anywhere in the story that her inability to have a child was the result of disobedience.

But one day years later when Sarah was 89 years old and Abraham was 99, they became lead players in an amazing drama. The biblical writer sets the stage at Abraham's tent among the oaks of Mamre, a few miles south and west of present-day Jerusalem.

It was high noon—the time of day when the heat was most intense—and Abraham was reclining in the shade of his tent. Suddenly, in the distance he saw three men coming toward their camp. In true oriental fashion he rushed out to greet them with a lavish show of Near Eastern hospitality.

Faith Is a Laughing Matter

After the visitors were fed and made comfortable, they settled down for conversation. It was probably then that Abraham began to feel his guests were not ordinary travelers. In the course of conversation, one guest said, "I shall visit you again next year without fail, and your wife will then have a son."

Apparently Sarah had been eavesdropping on the conversation from outside the tent. And when she heard the prediction that she would give birth to a baby at age 90, it was so ludicrous she laughed. After all, she hadn't conceived all during those years when it would have been normal for her to do so. Why would anyone think she would get pregnant now? No wonder she laughed!

And I'm glad she reacted the way she did. After all, Sarah could have responded in so many different ways. I could understand it if she had grumbled, "Fat chance!" Or she would have been justified in saying, "Don't give me any of that optimistic nonsense." If she had shown anger or unbelief or resentment, I wouldn't have been surprised. But instead, Sarah laughed.

It seems likely to me that her laughter was a grand mixture of belief and unbelief—half cynical, half hopeful, and half aghast. And if all those halves add up to more than a whole it's because that's the way we humans are. There is always incongruity in the way faith takes hold of the issues of life.

What Is a Giggle?

As I think back on the great faith-souls I've known, I find they all have one quality in common—the ability to laugh. They may have been separated by centuries in time and by vast differences in lifestyle and culture, but they were all laughers. Young or old, male or female, learned or untaught, they treated life with a special kind of laughter of joy. Sometimes it is the laughter of a battle won, but more often it is the mixed laughter of incredulity and wondrous expectation. At times it might even be described as an unself-conscious giggle.

In a way I hesitate to use the word giggle because it has received rather a bad name in our culture. I was quite interested in the definition of the word "giggle" in Samuel Johnson's two-hundred-year-old dictionary, "To laugh idly; to titter; to grin with merry levity. It is retained in Scotland." I'm not sure what that last sentence means, but I assume it meant that the Scots were known for their tendency to giggle.

Modern dictionaries are less kind in their definition. "To laugh in a silly, undignified way" is the way one dictionary words it. And then it goes on to identify a giggle with "juvenile or ill-concealed amusement, nervous embarrassment." I like Johnson's "merry levity" better. And while some giggling may be caused by nervousness, I'm inclined to believe that most of the time it is a spontaneous overflow of exuberance. Children giggle easily until the adult world convinces them it is foolish and inappropriate. Somehow, I believe, in our pseudo-sophistication we have lost some of the spontaneous charm and openness that our ancient Near Eastern ancestors of Abraham's time had. Our young children have it, too, until we dull their spontaneity as they grow older. This may well have been what Jesus meant when he told his listeners that unless they became like little children they couldn't be a part of his new society.

I have come to appreciate the word giggle because it doesn't seem to depend on structured humor or conventional logic. In a way, it is a spontaneous expression of faith which erupts from the feeling that all is well. I'm sure you've heard people say when someone giggles, "I don't see what you think is so funny." Of course, they don't. *They* fail to see anything funny because a giggle doesn't depend on a comedian, a plot, or an anecdote. Rather, it spills over from some inner spring of gladness—a feeling that all is well or it can be made well.

When the storyteller wrote that Sarah laughed, I'm inclined to think she probably giggled. After all—a baby at her age? But I don't get the impression that her laughter was the least bit cynical even though the visitor chided her for appearing to think that God couldn't work such a miracle. I have the feeling the Lord's messenger wasn't so much rebuking Sarah as reminding her that he understood her mixed feelings. In my imagination I can almost see him wagging his finger as he said, "You did too laugh."

Then, I think it is very significant that months later when the baby was born, Abraham and Sarah named him Isaac which means "laughter." It seems most likely that the baby's name had its beginnings in Sarah's response to the angel's announcement.

Hebrews' Hall of Faith

It is also significant, I believe, that the writer includes Sarah in his list of faith heroes and heroines in the eleventh chapter of Hebrews. This writer neither discredited her nor made light of her faith. Instead, we read that she "judged that he who had promised would keep the faith."

In the faith chapter in Hebrews no mention is made of Sarah's laughter when the angel visitor announced her coming pregnancy. Did the writer forget that part of her story or simply gloss over it? I know it is pure speculation, but I don't think so. Instead, I believe the retelling of the story in the setting of Hebrews 11 is proof somehow that Sarah's laughter was a faith reaction.

I have always enjoyed this story because Sarah's laughter illustrates so beautifully for me the quality of human faith. We are not single-minded, angelic creatures; we are intensely human. So much that happens to us threatens our ability to have faith. For this reason, most of the time we tend to receive God's Good News with a mixture of gladness and incredulity. If the mix is on the positive side, we laugh. But if our faith is weak, we're not able to laugh. Then, too, it is true, of course, that our laughter may not always be a shout of triumph. But it is the first and best step in that direction.

So often, though, in the hurly-burly of life we can hardly believe how far we've come, yet there's something in us that urges us on. That great Christian Walter Russell Bowie once told about an elderly man who said, "According to the calendar, I'm an oldish man, but a few days ago I played baseball with some boys and made a two-base hit. When I got to second, my breath was on first, but my heart was on third."

A first-century father presented this idea in poignant words. He had brought his epileptic son to Jesus' disciples for healing, but they couldn't do a thing for him. It was a pathetic case. The child suffered seizures that threw him to the ground, foaming at the mouth and grinding his teeth until he became rigid.

When the disciples couldn't help the boy, the father took his son to Jesus, and Jesus challenged him with these words, "If you believe, all things are possible to him who believes." With an anguished version of faith's laugh the father answered, "Lord, I believe; *help my unbelief.*"

It has always been reassuring to me that Jesus did not scorn or rebuke this father's wavering faith. And the Lord didn't send him home with instructions to come back when he was prepared to receive a miracle. Instead, Jesus responded to the best the father could offer at the moment, and healed the man's son.

Faith Is a Laughing Matter

Without being insensitive to this father's agony, I see laughter in his story. It's there in the incongruity of it all. If the father hadn't been so distraught and desperate, I think he would have interrupted what he was saying to laugh at himself. In response to Jesus' statement, he started, as we often do, to make a grand declaration of faith. But he had hardly begun his sentence, "I believe . . ." when, possibly even unconsciously, he realized it was almost too good to be true, and he added, "Please help my unbelief."

It seems to me that this father's honesty offers a prickly challenge to us in these closing years of the twentieth century. We Christians are often superpious and humorless. We take ourselves so seriously and believe that our notions and ideas are so "right." Sometimes we don't leave room for God to act and stretch our faith, nor do we make allowances for our own humanness. But, I believe that if we can recognize our frailties, and the sometimes perplexing incongruities of life, our faith will take on a healthy humor that may give rise to a giggle not unlike Sarah's.

Faith and Humor

The Jewish roots of our faith are rich in humor and laughter, even in the face of thousands of years of adversity. We would do well to model this response. More than any other race in history, the Jewish people have had to develop the kind of faith that retains the mood of laughter. Through centuries of indignities and persecution, they have survived by making light of the circumstances that were calculated to destroy them.

This is the mood of Tevye in *Fiddler on the Roof.* He has to struggle with a horse that goes lame, the collapse of beloved traditions, the inability of his wife to verbalize her love, and, worst of all, poverty. Tevye has every excuse to sit down and cry. Instead, he reasons with God. Sometimes he has a feeling that when things are too quiet in heaven, God thinks to himself, "What kind of mischief can I play on my friend Tevye?" Then Tevye explains that he's not really complaining, and with a humorous twist he adds, "After all, with your help, I'm starving to death." He agrees that it's no shame to be poor, "but it's no great honor either." And with that Tevye sings the line many remember best, "If I Were a Rich Man . . ."

This wonderful Jewish ability to blend laughter with dismay comes through in the Yiddish expression, *Oy!* Leo Rosten insists this is not a word, but a vocabulary—a lament, a protest, a cry of dismay, a reflex of delight. Lament and delight, both in the same word!

Another favorite Yiddish word, *gevalt,* has the same quality, as in "*Gevalt,* Lord, enough already!" Then comes the humor in the Yiddish proverb, "Man comes into the world with an *Oy!*—and leaves with a *gevalt!*" This kind of language and wisdom comes from a people who have suffered yesterday and realize they may suffer again tomorrow. But they are not victims as long as they can laugh, for laughter makes them conquerors. Faith is like that. It insists on surfacing even in the shadow of apparent doom and death.

As a matter of fact, faith does some of its best work in the environment of death—some kinds of death, at any rate. Death, after all, has many faces. It is not only the cessation of heart action nor of brain waves, as all of us know. It can be the death of a dream, or the death of separation (even temporary) from someone we love. Each disappointment has a touch of death about it, as does each hurt feeling. Sarah's problem, though, was a dead womb and a husband "as good as dead." But faith refuses to give up. Its belief may be mixed with unbelief, but something within a person of faith is strong enough to laugh and to expect better things tomorrow.

Faith Is a Laughing Matter

Ezekiel's Faith

The prophet Ezekiel was challenged to have that kind of faith. His nation was in captivity. They had lost heart and hope and had become accustomed to slavery. So God spread out a scene before Ezekiel's eyes that reflected not only the condition of his nation, but probably also Ezekiel's attitude toward their future prospects.

In his dream or vision Ezekiel saw a great valley of dry bones, the ultimate Death Valley. God asked the prophet, "Can these bones live?" In other words, can God bring life out of death, raise up a future out of bleached bones? Ezekiel answered, "O Lord God, thou knowest"—which is to say, "Why are you asking *me? You* understand such ultimates and absurdities better than I do."

But God wouldn't let Ezekiel off the hook quite that easily. True, only He knows such ultimates, but he also expects us to act as if we know that he knows. So God instructed Ezekiel to preach to the bones: "O dry bones, hear the word of the Lord."

Imagine! I can just hear Ezekiel say, "Lord, I feel like such a fool! I don't mind preaching, but this is ridiculous. They don't laugh at my jokes, they don't cry when I give a touching illustration, and they don't shout when I'm making a powerful point. And I keep wanting to look over my shoulder to see if some other preacher has followed me out here and is laughing himself silly at my carrying-on."

Somehow, I believe God wanted Ezekiel to laugh a little. The situation was too serious to face with cold logic; the prophet needed a breath of absurd gladness. And once Ezekiel began to preach, I can't help feeling that he punctuated his sermon with laughter—possibly a giggle. Then I can hear him say, "I'm such a fool, but it feels so good! I went to a seminary to master logic and the fine nuances of theology, and here I am preaching to bleached bones! If only my professors could see me now."

But as Ezekiel preached, something began to happen. At first he thought his imagination was getting the best of him—it sounded almost as if someone were applauding over to his left. But it wasn't applause; a toebone was joining to a footbone, and a kneebone with a thighbone. Imagine! I've often wondered whether Ezekiel ever finished that sermon. This may well have been one of the only sermons ever preached that didn't have an ending. But faith wrote a conclusion of its own: Where once that valley had been the resting place of bleached bones, now it hosted a mighty living mass of people.

Faith in Action

We can take courage in the truth that faith is active even at the place of death. It is at the deadly places in our lives that we are most likely to see faith in action—especially the kind of faith that, as Charles Wesley put it, "Laughs at impossibilities, and cries, it shall be done!"

Dmitrii Dudko, the courageous Russian Orthodox pastor in Moscow, is a kind of modern Ezekiel. One day during a dialog sermon he was challenged by someone in the audience who insisted that Dudko was deceiving himself in believing that religion could ever again flourish in Russia. Father Dudko pointed to the snow outside and said, "Snow still covers the ground, and there are still frosts. But Spring *is* possible." Then he continued, "There will be a religious Spring, and *everyone* is working toward it, believers and atheists alike."

Father Dudko's faith not only expects the "dead bones" to live again, he also believes that those who caused the death are themselves, unwittingly, working toward a grand

Faith Is a Laughing Matter

Resurrection. Like Sarah, who tried to keep her laughter hidden, Dudko must have laughed inwardly when he made that prediction. What a marvelous thought—the persons and the system who are trying so hard to destroy the Christian faith may actually be preparing the way for its greater glory! That's enough to tickle anyone's funnybone. But the up-to-date word that comes to us out of Russia validates Father Dudko's faith.

This tie between faith and joyful laughter is wonderful. John Wesley, the founder of Methodism, from the vantage point of two centuries seems to have been a rather grim and humorless man. He himself was indeed a tremendously self-disciplined man, and he insisted that those who worked with him be the same way. They were people with a *method* for achieving Christian holiness—they were "the people called Methodists." But he gave us one of theology's most memorable and unlikely sentences, "A laugh is half a prayer."

Of course it is. When we laugh, we are expressing the conviction that something is still right with the world, or if it isn't right at the moment, it will be some day. It is true, of course, that certain kinds of laughter are sometimes badly perverted. Tragically, none of God's gifts from sex to healing drugs has been free from perversion and abuse. But when laughter is used the way God intended it to be, we can know that God is enjoying it too.

A Singing Faith

While Wesley wouldn't necessarily get high marks as a standup comic, he knew how to enjoy and use humor. We see this in one of his definitions of a "Methodist": "He is therefore happy in God, yea, always happy . . . ." And while it is difficult to translate the humor of one generation to another, we can't help but smile at the "Directions for

Singing" that Wesley wrote for *Sacred Melody* in 1761: ". . . Sing lustily and with good courage. Beware of singing as if you were half dead or half asleep; but lift up your voice with strength. Be no more afraid of your voice now, nor more ashamed of its being heard, than when you sung the songs of Satan."

Then later on Wesley added: ". . . take care not to sing too slow. This drawling away naturally steals on all who are lazy; and it is high time to drive it out from us, and sing all our tunes just as quick as we did at first."

I just have to believe that Wesley had "tongue in cheek" as he laid down those rules. No wonder those early Methodists were known for their joyful and lusty singing!

One of the best evidences of the way John Wesley lived with laughter comes in a story from John Nelson, who traveled and preached with him in Cornwall for an extended period. For several weeks the two men had to sleep on a floor, using their coats for pillows. After nearly three weeks of this spartan life, Mr. Wesley awakened one morning about three o'clock. Turning over, he clapped Nelson on the side and said, "Brother Nelson, let us be of good cheer. I have one whole side yet, for the skin is off but one side!"

Nelson also remembered that they didn't have much to eat, and that the diet lacked variety. One morning, after preaching, Wesley stopped his horse to pick some blackberries. "Brother Nelson," he said, "we ought to be thankful that there are plenty of blackberries; for this is the best country I ever saw for getting a stomach, but the worst I ever saw for getting food." Wesley's faith was well-lined with laughter. He couldn't have managed without it.

Somehow I believe that more of our joy and laughter should be directed Godward. He is the true source of life's joy, and all true laughter has a divine quality. It affirms that the universe is God's, and that at some future time we, his children, will share in an all-encompassing heavenly victory.

In his letter to the Christians at Rome Paul wrote that the whole creation is groaning in travail as it waits for its future salvation (Rom. 8:22). That is true, and we see evidence on every side of the pain and travail in the natural world.

But the psalmist saw another side to that coin when he wrote, "Let the heavens rejoice, and let the earth be glad; let the sea roar, and the fulness thereof. Let the field be joyful, and all that is therein: then shall all the trees of the wood rejoice" (Ps. 96:11, 12 KJV). And the prophet Isaiah also wrote, "For ye shall go out with joy, and be led forth with peace: the mountains and the hills shall break forth before you into singing, and all the trees of the field shall clap their hands" (Isa. 55:12 KJV).

A Contagious Faith

In all of this we see that while nature may reflect its fallen state because of sin by being "red in tooth and claw," it also points to the Creator. Indeed nature reflects joy and laughter. From the trill of the bird to the wagging tail of the dog and the seemingly erratic scamperings of a squirrel we catch the laughter theme. And it is contagious as well as healing.

In August 1964 Norman Cousins, Editor of *Saturday Review,* flew home from abroad with a slight fever. Within a week his condition had deteriorated so badly that he was hospitalized. After tests, he was diagnosed as suffering from a serious collagen illness, and a specialist predicted that he had one chance in five hundred for a complete recovery.

But Norman Cousins had a strong will to live. He became convinced that his own body chemistry was a major factor in his recovery. And he believed that his body chemistry would be enhanced by vigorously exercising affirmative emotions. Cousins next concluded that there was no better way to do this than through laughter. But he frankly admitted to himself that there was nothing less funny than being flat on his back in severe pain.

So, Mr. Cousins laid out a systematic program of activities that would produce laughter. Allan Funt, the producer of the "Candid Camera" television series, sent over some of the best and funniest of the films from that show. And from another source Mr. Cousins obtained some of the old Marx Brothers films. And in between pictures his nurse would often read to him from humor books.

"I made the joyous discovery," he writes in his wonderful book entitled *The Anatomy of Illness,* "that ten minutes of genuine laughter had an anesthetic effect and would give me at least two hours of pain-free sleep."

A skeptic might argue that Cousins had psyched himself to sleep. But medical science supported his thinking. During a routine illness a patient's sedimentation rate would be around 30 to 40, but during Mr. Cousins's first week in the hospital it had shot up to 115, an extremely serious level. But when the "humor treatment" was started, the sedimentation readings responded favorably. In fact, after each period of laughter the rate dropped at least five points, and while the drop wasn't large, it held and was cumulative.

While it is true, of course, that Mr. Cousins's final recovery involved several elements, he considers his periods of laughter a major factor. What he experienced, and to a degree it can be measured scientifically, was put into a classic phrase by a biblical writer twenty-five or more centuries ago, "A cheerful heart is a good medicine, but a downcast spirit dries up the bones" (Prov. 17:22). *Today's English Version* is still stronger, "Being cheerful keeps you healthy. It is slow death to be gloomy all the time."

Faith's Healing Factor

The writers of Proverbs didn't necessarily try to make a religious point in all of their maxims. More often they simply reported on life as it was. This particular writer had discovered that a cheerful heart had a healing quality, and those who laugh are on their way to faith—the two are intertwined.

But in spite of our glorious faith-heritage of almost 2,000 years, most of us are still guilty of acting like Sarah—we're excited to think that life might come out of the deadness of today's hurt, disappointment, or hopelessness, but we find it almost too good to be true. We're a lot like the father in the Gospel story who said, "Lord, I believe," but who then was suddenly engulfed by the awareness that his supply of faith was so small as compared to the enormity of his struggle. He then added honestly, "Help my unbelief."

Most of us offer the Lord a mixed bag of belief and unbelief. But in his wonderful generosity God accepts both our faith and our doubts, and I suspect he welcomes our mixed offering with joy—and possibly even a laugh.

We began this chapter with Janis. Now, I'm happy to report that she has applied this "laugh therapy" in her own life with considerable success. Things still aren't easy for her, and nearly every day she is confronted with a variety of concerns and problems. But she meets them with the joy of the Lord—her hidden strength—and Timmy continues to amaze everyone with his progress.

Even though each day is a struggle, Janis continues to turn life's unpromising stuff into victory. "You've heard about those folks who laugh all the way to the bank?" she asks. "I'm way ahead of them. Even without the bank, I'm laughing all the way." That is faith!

. . . there are those who treat life with resignation. They speak often of fate—a word that the ear easily confuses with faith. But it is exactly the opposite. When we believe in fate, we seldom exercise faith. The two simply don't go together. A belief in fate assumes that whatever will be, will be. But faith believes that change is possible. Even more than that, it releases the energy to make change happen.

{ 2 }

Faith Comes with Our Original Equipment

Several years ago I was in New York City on a bitter winter afternoon and was scheduled for a flight back to our home which was then in Wisconsin. I had an important meeting early the next morning, so I needed desperately to get an afternoon or early evening flight. But when I checked in at the midtown airline terminal, I was told there wouldn't be a New York to Chicago flight at all, either in the afternoon or that night. The temperature was hovering just a little above zero, the skies were turbulent—a storm front had closed in on the city.

Being slow to take good advice, I went out to the airport anyway, hoping there might be a change in the weather. After waiting for several hours, I was pleased to hear an announcement which stated that a plane would be leaving for Chicago in a couple of hours if the weather cleared just a little bit more.

I was elated, but also somewhat apprehensive. If only one airline were willing to fly that night, I couldn't help but wonder about the safety factor. But I decided to risk it.

To kill time and ease a hungry feeling, I went to a standup lunch counter for a hot dog. While I was eating, I noticed an airline pilot nearby. Since we were the only patrons at the counter, I struck up a conversation with him and learned that he was the pilot scheduled for my Chicago flight. We talked about the bad weather and the precautionary measures airlines took under such circumstances. The conversation eased my mind considerably, and I felt reassured when I learned that his home was in Chicago and he was as anxious to get there as I was.

When the announcer called the flight an hour or so later, the weather still seemed threatening, but when we boarded, I settled back in my seat with complete calm. We took off on schedule and the flight was uneventful. For this I was deeply grateful to God and an experienced pilot.

Everyday Faith

For me, this was a faith experience. While it was not a dramatic one like being saved from a plane crash, it was the kind of everyday faith experience that we are inclined to take for granted. I have no idea, of course, whether any of my fellow passengers that night viewed our safe flight as a faith event the way I did. Or if they did, it is possible most of them would have used the word "faith" to describe their confidence only in the pilot and the airline.

So often people without a living and vital faith in God seem embarrassed to ever use what they would think of as religious language to describe their feelings. Instead, they might resort to a generalized term like, "I just felt good about it all." And if you were to ask them to be more specific, it's likely they would shrug their shoulders and say, "Oh, *you* know."

As a matter of fact, we *do* know. Whether we use the word "faith" or not, it is very much a part of our daily experience. In fact, we can't survive without it. It is as essential to life as the air we breathe because while air keeps us

THE POWER OF BELIEVING

alive physically, it is faith that keeps us going emotionally and spiritually. Edna St. Vincent Millay understood this when she wrote:

> Not Truth, but Faith, it is
> That keeps the world alive.

Frequently, we think of faith as something mystical and ethereal—something possessed by just a few saintly people. But as a matter of fact, it is a common commodity that every human being has and uses every day.

Theologians speak of "common grace." By this they mean that every person benefits from the grace of God in some measure—even possibly without knowing it. For example, when Jesus commented that God sends his rain on the just and the unjust, that is common grace.

I think of faith the same way. It is a common product available in its natural form to everyone and is used a thousand times a day by "believers" and "unbelievers" alike. When I was reflecting on the meaning of faith, I turned to the dictionary. Mine defines faith as "Confidence or trust in persons or things; belief which is not based on proof." That made sense to me as I thought about the kind of faith we use every day.

When we go to bed at night, we have faith to believe that we'll wake up in the morning. When I take a nonstop elevator to the thirty-eighth floor of a downtown office building, I exercise a lot of faith. I haven't the faintest notion how or why an elevator works. I know, of course, that millions of people ride up and down in elevators every day, but this doesn't necessarily mean that my particular elevator is going to function properly. It is true the inspection sticker by the door indicates the elevator was checked, but that was several months ago. And I can't even read the name of the inspector! But, by faith, I walk through the door, punch the button for the thirty-eighth floor, and settle back with confidence. I believe I'll get there and that the door will open at the right time.

Some Facts about Faith

At one time or another most of us have had to place our faith in the hands of doctors. I recall a time several years ago when I was wheeled into the operating room of the hospital. While they were making final preparations for surgery, one of the nurses identified herself as a roommate of an old friend. While we were talking, the anesthesiologist said he was going to give me an injection. "It won't hurt," he promised, and it didn't. But suddenly I was caught in the middle of a sentence, and I couldn't finish it. In that split second two thoughts raced through my mind: I must look foolish with my mouth hanging open and unable to finish what I'd been saying . . . and I was completely under the control of the people around me—none of whom I had known five minutes before. I had to have faith that they knew what they were doing—and that I would make it through all right.

Then, too, it takes faith to get married. And it takes a lot of faith to have children! Who knows what will happen five, ten, fifteen years down the road, but we have faith that everything will work out in an acceptable and satisfactory way. Then on the more mundane level, it takes faith to open a can of soup or to eat in a restaurant. We have to have faith that the can of soup has been properly prepared and inspected by a trustworthy manufacturer and that the restaurant is clean and reliable and we won't be poisoned by bad food.

Now, any person who doesn't have the kind of common

faith I've been describing cannot help but be victimized by penetrating fears—phobias such as fear of people, heights, germs, dirt, the dark. One way or another these are fears common to most of us, but when they get out of balance we lose the measure of common faith that makes living possible. Such phobias are illnesses. They aren't natural to us and they rob us of the ordinary faith by which we manage to live every day.

A Natural Faith?

I suspect, though, we are all born with a natural faith. After all, doesn't a baby trust implicitly? And isn't it the process of disappointment and deception—including playful deception—that gradually conditions us to become doubters?

In a nontheological way I believe that faith is native to us. On the other hand, doubting is a learned reaction. If we lived in a setting where we were never deceived, we would never doubt. In a sense, then, the business of Christianity is to restore us to the state of believing. Except, of course, our believing operates in a world where sin exists. This simply means that we must know what to believe and what to reject.

As with all of God's gifts, faith can be used negatively as well as positively. Sitting on the ashheap of his dreams Job complained, "The thing I feared most has come upon me." His reverse faith had worked. Job had expected something bad to happen—he had faith that it would—and it did, just as he had anticipated.

This is the back side, the demonic side, of faith, and all of us are familiar with it. I met a friend one day just after someone had left an ugly dent in her Ford LTD bought only a month before. "I just knew this was going to happen," she said. "You work and save to get something nice, and you can be sure that it's only a matter of time until something happens to mess it up. You can count on it."

A Negative Faith?

This lady had a well-developed negative faith. But if she had turned the same energy to trust in God, or merely to a secular expectation of happiness, she might have surrounded herself with joy and well-being.

While I believe in faith healing, I see far more evidence around me of faith *sickness*. So many of us court illness by our expectation of it. A friend of mine who is a Christian Scientist once told me that he wouldn't watch certain patent medicine commercials which are so much a part of television. "When you see those little hammers pounding on your forehead in the headache commercial, or the miseries of the digestive system in graphic color in the antacid ad, you're being mentally conditioned for sickness and pain."

When I first heard that comment, I smiled, partly because my friend was smiling. But then I realized he wasn't joking. What he was saying wasn't at all funny, especially when we remember that the time such commercials usually appear is during the dinner hours. And that is a time when our bodies need nothing but positive influences.

Lois Gould describes this kind of negative faith in her novel, *Such Good Friends*. For years a character in the story had been convinced that he would have cancer. His wife said of him, "His living faith rested firmly on the notion that something terrible was just about to happen." She further explained that even on a bright, sunny day he would predict a storm for the next day. And then when his prediction failed, he wasn't the least bit happy about being wrong. Usually we label this attitude as unbelief or doubt. But actually, it is misdirected faith—faith in something that doesn't deserve our faith.

Then, once we put this negative faith to work, it begins accumulating evidence to support its case. The hypochondriac hears the symptoms of a fatal disease, finds a smidgin of pain in the right spot, and soon is working out the details for his funeral service. And you don't have to be a full-fledged neurotic to follow this pattern. How often have we awakened with a cold and complained, "When I sat next to that woman last night who was wheezing and sneezing, I just knew I'd catch it." Of course, there were some germs at work, but it isn't likely they would have won the day without some help from their cooperative, negative prospect.

Norman Cousins, former editor of *Saturday Review* and the author of that marvelous book entitled *Anatomy of an Illness,* is somewhat critical of the medical profession for the negative influence doctors sometimes exert on their patients. On the tenth anniversary of the illness he writes about in his book he happened to see one of the specialists who had predicted that he would be the victim of progressive paralysis. On seeing him, the doctor's surprise was obvious. And when they shook hands, Cousins purposely increased the pressure until the doctor winced and asked to be released. Then the doctor said that he could tell from the handshake that Cousins was well. Then he asked just what had happened.

"It all began," Cousins responded, "when I decided that some experts don't really know enough to make a pronouncement of doom on a human being." Then he went on to express the hope that doctors would be more careful

Faith Comes with Our Original Equipment

about what they say to their patients, for "they might be believed and that could be the beginning of the end."* Such is the power of negative faith.

Overcoming Negative Faith

Unfortunately, we are inclined to exercise this kind of unbelief in almost any area of our lives. If we move into a social setting expecting people to be unfriendly, it generally turns out that way because of our own negative attitude. A salesperson knows that if he or she expects rejection, this is exactly what will happen and the sale will be missed.

In a football game if a quarterback throws an interception, he knows he'd better try another pass just as soon as possible to avoid a negative attitude. And the baseball player who is in a slump discovers that his worst enemy is the negative voice telling him he is going to strike out again or hit into a double play. Yes, the things we fear most happen to us because we subvert the magnificent power of faith. So often, we put more faith in misery than in victory and concentrate more on hell than on heaven. There is little doubt—that which we fear the most usually happens.

Focusing Faith

But there's another side to this that offers us a glimmer of hope. If we have the faith to expect the worst, we already have the basic raw product to bring about the best. Our problem is not that we lack faith, but that we focus our faith on the wrong object. Actually, some of the greatest believers I've ever known are concentrating their faith on the

*Norman Cousins, *Anatomy of an Illness* (New York: W. W. Norton and Company, 1979), 159–160.

wrong things. And some of them, sad to say, are Christians. They mean well, but they've concentrated for so long on the dark side of life, rather than on Christ and his goodness, that they constantly expect the worst. And by their expecting, they help bring it to pass. They have the faith; the need is to change its focus.

That focus is completely converted in the lives of the persons listed in the eleventh chapter of Hebrews. The faith of those people was firmly fixed in God. When that happens, all the rest of life enjoys the overflow. Our work, our relationships, and our physical health all enjoy a more positive position because the focus of our faith is right.

But there's also an important dynamic at work here. Not only do those who put their faith in God benefit, but everyone around them is better off as well. Jesus described his followers as the "salt of the earth" because of their potential to flavor and influence everyone around them and society as a whole. God's "faith people" are a contagious lot. The lives they touch in any given day receive a certain measure of redemptive faith from them.

I know you've experienced this as I have—some Christians are so "faith-possessed" that one can feel the nearness of God simply by being with them. But even the average Christian is a source of strength, whether he or she knows it or not and whether others are willing to acknowledge it. In fact, I just have to believe that even some cynical secularists are sustained to a degree by the influence of Christians in the world around them without ever realizing it.

Now, if faith is such a common element in all of life, and if we can exercise it in a self-destructive manner (as we frequently do), then I think it is important for us to explore it in relation to God—its true source. What does the Bible have to say about faith in God?

Defining Faith

Although faith is a major theme throughout both the Old and the New Testaments, only in one place does the Bible give us a specific definition, "Now faith is the substance of things hoped for, the evidence of things not seen" (Heb. 11:1). It's interesting to see that the writer of this biblical definition of faith doesn't bother to use any exclusively religious words. Actually, these same words could be used by a secular philosopher as easily as by a devout believer in Christ. This underlines all the more emphatically the idea that faith is a common commodity, and that it is up to us to decide whether or not we will focus it on God, the true author of faith.

I've always liked the imaginative way this faith-definition is handled in the Centenary translation, "Faith is the title deed of things hoped for." A title deed insures ownership.

It was "title deed faith" that kept Abraham and Sarah going through all of the years of their pilgrimage—from Ur to Haran to Canaan to Egypt and back to Canaan again. In speaking of Abraham the writer to the Hebrews said that "he looked forward to the city which has foundations, whose builder and maker is God" (Heb. 11:10). Now, Abraham had never seen or moved into that "city," but he had the title deed to it because of God's promise. Through faith, Abraham owned it.

The cynical person sometimes accuses the faith-pilgrim of being unrealistic. "You believe in dreams," he says, "but I'm a realist." Actually, though, none of us sees life realistically—with pure objectivity. All of us view life through our own attitudes, philosophy, or prejudices. Our outlook on life is filtered through our perceptions and our history.

Some people exist day after day in a climate of despair. Whatever happens to them is viewed through their despair lens. What these people call "realism" is actually nothing more than pessimism.

Faith—or Fate?

Then there are those who treat life with resignation. They speak often of fate—a word that the ear easily confuses with faith. But it is exactly the opposite. When we believe in fate, we seldom exercise faith. The two simply don't go together. A belief in fate assumes that whatever will be, will be. But faith believes that change is possible. Even more than that, it releases the energy to make change happen.

From this we see that faith is a particular way of looking at life—even as is materialism, despair, or resignation. Faith doesn't ignore or deny facts, but it interprets them through prior convictions. Each of us interprets a particular situation through the attitudes that shape our lives.

George Bernard Shaw was generally a kind of irreligious curmudgeon, but he gave us any number of insights worthy of the faith that nurtured his generation in England. He illuminated the idea of faith in magnificent lines that later became popular in American politics, "You see things as they are; and you ask, 'Why?' But I dream things that never were; and I ask, 'Why not?'"

There in a sentence is the contrast between the despairing outlook and the faith outlook. Both confront the same situations, but despairing persons wring their hands and ask "Why?" This kind of questioning rarely solves any problems. If anything, it makes them more frightening and unsolvable.

The American poet, Edwin Arlington Robinson, once wrote these words to a friend, "Everything is all stirred up here at home, and I am living on hope and faith, which, by the way, make a pretty good diet when the mind will receive them." Yes, faith always has high expectations, and it acts to bring them to pass. As the nineteenth-century American philosopher, William James, put it, "Believe that life is worth living and your belief will help create the fact."

Bruce Larson tells about a doctor in Denver who had specialized in the physician-patient relationship. He had a patient suffering from cancer of the prostate that had metastasized to the skull, hips, and spine. "Medically speaking, the man had at most four weeks to live. His doctor told him, 'If you believe this cancer is terminal, it will be. You and I will go into a partnership. I'll give you everything medicine knows—surgery, estrogen, whatever is needed. I want you to have the best time of your life: laugh, do what you want to do, begin to see it as funny.' Today that man is alive."*

The doctor wasn't being unrealistic, and he didn't demand unrealism of his patient. Both of them knew the facts, and the facts weren't good. But the doctor chose to view the facts from a positive vantage point, rather than a negative one, and he helped his patient to *change the facts*. Facts, after all, are nothing more than an accumulation of data, and they are usually open to change as new information becomes available. It is faith which provides some of the new data.

A Soldier's Faith

On one occasion Jesus said that the most alive faith he'd seen was in a Roman soldier. The event that prompted this observation occurred when Jesus was on the road to Capernaum. The soldier, a centurion, appealed to Jesus on behalf of his servant at home who was paralyzed.

*Bruce Larson, *There's a Lot More to Health Than Not Being Sick* (Waco, Texas: Word Books, 1981), 138.

THE POWER OF BELIEVING

In response to the soldier's concern Jesus volunteered to travel on to the man's house and heal the servant. But the centurion was a Gentile, and he knew that according to Jewish law Jesus would be defiled—unclean—if he entered his home. So, instead, the centurion said, "Lord, I am not worthy to have you come under my roof; but only say the word, and my servant will be healed" (Matt. 8:8).

Matthew concludes the story with these words, "When Jesus heard him, he marveled, and said to those who followed him, 'Truly, I say unto you, not even in Israel, have I found such faith'" (Matt. 8:10). In other words, not even God's chosen people had faith equal to this Gentile soldier. What was the difference, and what made this centurion think this way?

A centurion, as the name indicates, was an officer over one hundred men. These officers were the backbone of the Roman army. They were the men in the middle who received commands from their superiors and relayed them to the men in their units. As part of a chain of command, centurions had ultimate respect for the power of authority.

It was this army background that gave the centurion the rare insight to understand Jesus' authority over the servant's paralysis. In effect the centurion was saying something like this in Matthew 8:9, "I know power when I see it, and I understand the chain of command. I'm under authority; the generals send their orders down to me. And I have authority: I say to a man, 'Go,' and he goes.

"Now I can see the chain of command in this situation. Sickness is giving orders to my servant, and he has to obey because the sickness is more powerful than he is. But you, Jesus, are higher in the rank of authority than sickness is. If you say to the sickness, 'Go,' it will have to go. That's the kind of authority you have. And you don't have to come to

Faith Comes with Our Original Equipment

my unworthy house to exercise it. You command, and it will happen."

This Roman officer had his world in order. He knew God was in control. He didn't close his eyes to the paralysis that was destroying his servant; he could see its power at work. But he also knew there was an authority in the universe superior to the authority of that illness. He saw it in the power of God that was being demonstrated through Jesus.

I've always been impressed by how much Jesus liked this centurion's faith. As far as I can see, this Roman soldier wasn't a conventionally religious man, and, yet, he was showing more and better faith than any Jew Jesus had seen—and that may even have included his own disciples.

The point is—yes, the centurion had a generic, common kind of faith that everyone had, but it was focused in the right direction! And that is what made his faith different from the rest. He could see the power of his servant's paralysis, but he could also see the superior power of Jesus. His faith was in Jesus rather than in the illness.

The Focus of Our Faith

The writer of Hebrews says in effect: the person who wants to please God will have to believe that God *is* and rewards those who seek him (11:6). This simply means that we need to turn our capacity for faith toward the only One who, in the end, fully merits such an investment from us. And we believe not only that God exists. We also believe he is *good,* and that he responds to us.

When John G. Paton, the early Christian missionary to the New Hebrides, set out to translate the New Testament for the people of the South Sea Islands, he couldn't find a way to get across the idea of believing. There was no word in their language that really conveyed that idea. After struggling for some time to translate the verse in Acts where Paul and Silas told the Philippian jailer to "Believe on the Lord Jesus Christ and you will be saved," Dr. Paton finally came up with this solution, "Lean your whole weight upon the Lord Jesus Christ and be saved."

There was no better way to say it. To believe God is to lean *all* of our weight on him. But someone might say, "But if I lean my whole weight, I'll fall if the support fails." Right! And that's exactly what we mean by "faith." Faith is betting our lives on the strength and character of God. We dare to believe that he is strong enough to see us through, whether life is stormy or calm.

That's faith. It's part of the original equipment God gave us. And yet, ironically, we have to relearn how to focus it on God—back where it really belongs. Somehow, the Roman centurion on the road to Capernaum, without any biblical background and out of a pagan heritage, managed to do just that.

Malcolm Muggeridge was an international journalist for many years, and for four years he was editor of *Punch,* the English humor magazine, before going into broadcast journalism. From all outward appearances he was the epitome of success, and yet he titled his autobiography *Chronicles of Wasted Years.*

But relatively late in life this distinguished journalist awakened to faith in God. In his marvelous little book, *Something Beautiful for God,* he contemplates the change in his expectations as he looks out of a window on a wintry countryside, "The bees and the badgers are asleep; the birds perch hungrily on the bare twigs; nature seems dead forever. Yet not so. Faith tells me that soon the badgers and the bees will be awake, the trees load themselves with leaves. . . ."

Faith Comes with Our Original Equipment

Here Muggeridge refers to "a faith easily held. We know—or think we do—that spring will always return." This is what I have referred to as a generic or common faith. But then Muggeridge goes on to speak of a faith with a God-focus, ". . . the interior of my heart seems a dead landscape. Yet faith tells me that it, likewise, can have a spring in the rebirth promised to us all in the new dispensation which Christ brought to the world. The old envies budding with holy love; the old lusts burning with spiritual appetite; the old hopes and desires finding a new destination in the bright radiance of God's universal love."*

The Good News of our faith is that sunshine and laughter await us. All we need to do is begin to direct our faith toward God—its true home!

---

*Malcolm Muggeridge, *Something Beautiful for God* (London: William Collins), 138–139.

. . . God knows all about our goodness struggles and he doesn't judge us based on goodness. Instead, God does the fair and generous thing—he judges us based on the one thing we all have in common. Built into all human beings is the capacity for faith, and it is up to us to choose whether that faith is directed toward God or toward evil. We are all faith-inclined, and we all choose the object of that faith.

3

Why Is Faith So Important?

THE MAN HAD HEARD ONE SERMON TOO MANY on the same subject. "Believe, believe, believe," he complained. "You'd think nothing else mattered but believing. Why is faith such a big deal?"

I didn't blame him for being upset, and I didn't know his pastor, so I had no way of knowing whether his complaint was justified. But I understood his problem. The Bible seems to put an unreasonable emphasis on faith. For example, the writer of the letter to the Hebrews puts it this way, "*Without faith it is impossible to please him* (God)" (11:6, italics mine). That sounds terribly final. "Impossible" rules out all other considerations. It makes it sound as if nothing but faith matters.

If this were the only verse to give faith such unique importance, we might reason our way around it. But the same idea can be found in any number of other places. When a father came to Jesus with a desperate appeal for his son to be healed, Jesus answered, "Everything is possible to one who has faith." The promise is so all-inclusive—*everything*—and it narrows down to such a singular requirement: *faith.*

Jesus said the same sort of thing to his disciples. When they couldn't help a person who had asked for their assistance, Jesus not only rebuked their lack of faith, he told

Why Is Faith So Important?

them how little was needed to work miracles. If you have faith like a grain of mustard seed, Jesus said, you can move "mountains." The figure of speech is dramatic at both ends. What could be more immovable than a mountain and what could be a smaller cause than a tiny mustard seed?

For the disciple who might complain, "I have so little faith," Jesus was saying, "See how much you can do with even a little!" They probably had enough already, if only they were willing to use it. The point here is that we fail, not because our stock of faith is so small. Rather, we fail because we don't use the faith we have.

In one of the darkest days in the history of Israel, the prophet Habakkuk struggled to understand the meaning of God's dealings with his nation. When at last the answer came to him, I'm sure it wasn't the one he expected: "The just shall live by faith," God told him. Unfortunately, these words are so much a part of our religious vocabulary that they don't shock us the way they should.

The Just Shall Live by Faith

In reality, it seems to me it would have made more sense if God had told Habakkuk that "the just should live by *goodness.*" After all, if someone is "just," isn't it his goodness and character that make him acceptable to God? But, no, the prophet-writer insists, "The *just* shall live by faith" (italics mine). As we reflect on this assertion, we begin to see that unless the "just"—those persons who have been made right before God by accepting Christ as their Savior—have faith, they will lose their ability to live godly lives. We must have faith if we are to live rich, full, and holy lives.

Centuries later, Paul quoted Habakkuk's insight in his letter to the Roman Christians to explain the Good News of salvation through Christ. And we know from Paul's story that he hadn't known this truth until his experience of meeting Jesus on the Damascus road. Before that, as a good Jew and Pharisee, he had counted on the Law to save him. But now he knew that his justness needed a deeper foundation: *faith*. And so, the message in all of Paul's letters was that keeping the Law doesn't save us—personal achievement isn't the answer. We are saved by *grace*.

Time after time, Jesus gave the same explanation to people who came to him for healing. There's almost a monotony to his words, "Your faith has made you whole." It is almost as if Jesus minimized his part in the healing transaction. It's as if he were saying to the grateful person, "Don't thank me. It was your faith that did it."

At the same time Jesus never gave credit to some of those things that the sick and needy might have thought they had going for themselves. At no point did Jesus say, "You're one of the most deserving people I've met." Instead, he insisted that the only qualification for their healing was faith. He never suggested that anything else played a part in the results.

In all probability we would have liked for Jesus to have given a more sophisticated and dramatic explanation. Instead, his analysis of what happened was so simple that it's almost abrupt: it was their faith and nothing more that did it.

Heroes of the Faith?

It would be hard to explain many of the Old Testament heroes and heroines without faith. God seemed to use the strangest folks! Two brothers, Cain and Abel, brought their offerings to God. God accepted one and rejected the other. From our point of view, God's action seems rather arbitrary. But the writer of the book of Hebrews says that it was perfectly logical: it was "by faith" that Abel offered "a more excellent sacrifice than Cain."

Noah was a good man, but when the New Testament

Why Is Faith So Important?

writer analyzes Noah's secret, he says it was faith that made him great. By our standards, Abraham sometimes ran close to the borderline of honesty, but in the total evaluation of his character, he was judged by his faith.

Rahab had probably lived a pretty seamy life in the city of Jericho until she met the Israelite spies; she operated a shady hotel and was a prostitute. Yet when the armies of Israel conquered Jericho, Rahab and her family were the only ones spared. But not only was her life saved, she eventually married a Hebrew and became one of Jesus' ancestors. The writer of the letter to the Hebrews says all of this happened because of her faith—certainly at the time she didn't have much else going for her.

I've mentioned only a few of many scriptures that emphasize the importance of faith, but we can see from these that the Bible portrays faith as the key factor in our relationship with God. But why? Why should faith be more important than love or goodness?

Faith in Paradise

In its picturesque and profound way, the Book of Genesis tells us that faith is the basis for all of our decision-making. Our choices, large or small, are faith choices. In the beginning the human race had a setting so ideal that it was called Eden—paradise. Eden had everything a person could ever need or want: food for the body, beauty to satisfy our aesthetic hunger, human fellowship to meet our need for intellectual and social interchange, and communion with God to fulfill the desires of the spirit.

But there was one forbidden object in the garden, the tree of knowledge of good and evil. Adam and Eve were told they must never eat the fruit of that tree because if they did, they would die.

One day, according to the story, a subtle voice spoke to

the woman, and through her to the man. The voice asked, "Did God say, 'You shall not eat of any tree of the garden'?" When Eve replied, she said, "We may eat of the fruit of the trees of the garden; but God said, 'You shall not eat of the fruit of the tree which is in the midst of the garden, neither shall you touch it, lest you die'" (Gen. 3:1–3).

The alien voice had raised two questions about the character of God. First, is he good? The voice implied that he wasn't or he wouldn't have refused them anything. Second, is God truthful? And the voice indicated that he wasn't—God was lying when he warned them that failure to comply would cause death.

So, Adam and Eve chose not to believe God. It's as simple as that. However you want to describe or analyze their conduct, in the end it comes down to this—they didn't have faith in God. A choice was put sharply before them—to believe God or to believe the voice. They chose to believe the alien voice. It is sometimes said that their sin was one of disobedience, but their waywardness came from a faith-choice. They wouldn't have disobeyed if they had *believed* God.

Is God Good?

Faith in God still comes down to the same issues that were raised in the Garden of Eden: Is God good, and is he telling us the truth about the nature of life and the universe? Unfortunately, all too often we respond much as Adam and Eve did. And God still suffers from the bad press he received from the Eden story—he's pictured as mean and vindictive, and if we don't do what pleases him, life will be miserable because he will be out to get us.

So many people have a negative impression of God— he'll get you if you don't watch out. But if God was like that,

Why Is Faith So Important?

I believe he would have created the world in black and white or a drab gray. But the opposite is true. God has given us a world of living color with an infinite variety of shades. Those of us who live in the upper part of the Midwest and East are especially reminded of this in the fall of the year when the trees become a flame of living color. And then again in the spring we witness a grand resurrection as the trees become green again and the fields and roadsides burst out with wildflower brilliance.

There is something terribly illogical about what Adam and Eve did. Even though they had every reason to know that God was good and would provide for them, they chose to believe the alien and sinister voice that questioned the goodness of God. Unfortunately, though, even in our enlightened times we are victimized by the same lack of faith. There is so much evidence around us, even in our most difficult moments, that love is better than hate, that purity is better than filth, that integrity is better than deceit—yet all too often we *choose* not to believe, not to trust God.

In fact, I believe that sin is a bad faith-choice. For example, if I hate, I'm choosing—whether I realize it or not—to *believe* in hate instead of love. To lie is to believe that falsehood is better than truth. When I speak unkindly of someone else, I'm choosing to put my faith in destructive words instead of gracious, loving, and generous words. And if I let my mind wander around in the gutter or burn with resentment, I have made a deliberate choice against purity and forgiveness.

Trust without Reservation

I've heard Elton Trueblood, that much loved Quaker philosopher, say, "Faith is not belief without proof, but trust without reservation." There's plenty of proof on the side of faith. But faith requires us to bet our lives on what we believe. It asks us to "trust without reservation." But the irony is this—we're so often ready to put that kind of trust in unworthy and unlikely ideas. Like Adam and Eve, we seem to find it all too easy to believe the alien voice, even though there is so much around us that speaks of God's goodness and beauty.

But since, as we've seen, faith is behind all of our decision-making, behind everything that determines our actions and reactions, it is in reality the finest and noblest gift we can give to God—it is the gift of ourselves.

I remember so well the story that impressed itself upon my mind in my early childhood. It concerned the Indian chief who wanted to become a Christian. In an effort to obtain forgiveness and satisfaction he offered the Lord his hunting equipment, his saddle, his horse. But none of these offerings brought satisfaction or made him feel forgiven. Finally, in desperation, he looked up and said to God, "Big chief gives you himself." And with that faith-commitment he felt forgiven and accepted. This was the gift that mattered to God.

Faith Doesn't Depend on One's IQ

As a young pastor in my first church, I recall meeting a retarded man on my first Sunday. He appeared to be around fifty years old. I noticed that everyone treated him as if he were a very young boy. I soon learned that he had never been invited to join the church because everyone assumed he was incapable of participating in the usual preparation classes. Because of this, Emil's attendance had been limited pretty much to the Sunday school hour.

For some reason, though, Emil began to attend our regular worship service, and I noticed that he listened closely to my sermons. This was encouraging to me because I felt I was speaking simply enough for him to understand.

After a time when we got better acquainted I talked with Emil about his love for God and invited him to join the church. He was delighted and after further instruction he became a church member for the first time.

God didn't require any kind of intelligence test or explanation of doctrine. If he had, Emil would never have made it. But he had faith enough to please God. In fact, Emil's faith may have been sufficiently childlike and uncluttered that it was better and stronger than my own. What a marvelous wideness in God's mercy!

Faith and Goodness

At the same time, I'm glad we don't have to pass a goodness test to be accepted by God. I'm glad Hebrews 11:6 doesn't read, "And without *goodness* it is impossible to please him." Now, I'm all for goodness, but let's face it, none of us deserves a blue ribbon for goodness—not all of us start out from the same place in the goodness department.

I was reminded of this fact one Sunday when I was officiating at the dedication and baptism of two babies, each of whom had an entirely different spiritual heritage. One baby came from a long line of beautiful people. His parents, grandparents, and great-grandmother were all dedicated Christian people. And I knew that his ancestors were gracious and honorable folk. It was obvious this little fellow had a real headstart in life.

But the other little fellow was already running on a slow track. Even though his parents seemed to try hard, they didn't appear, on the surface at least, to be any better than was absolutely necessary. And his grandparents left a whole lot to be desired in the good living department.

THE POWER OF BELIEVING

I couldn't help but think as I looked at those two innocent little ones that each of them might well grow up with a different understanding of goodness. But then I was reminded that goodness as such would not be the standard for their acceptance by God.

This truth has also caused me to be a little more patient with grumpy people, especially when I learn that they come from a long line of grumps. I sometimes wonder if grumpiness isn't partly hereditary—maybe people have grumpy blood. At the same time there may be environmental qualities in being grumpy—a grump learns to be grumpy from the people around him. But however a grump gets grumpy, I have noticed that it seems harder for them to be good—at least by our standards. But I have to believe that God knows all about our goodness struggles and he doesn't judge us based on goodness.

Instead, God does the fair and generous thing—he judges us based on the one thing we all have in common. Built into all human beings is the capacity for faith, and it is up to us to choose whether that faith is directed toward God or toward evil. We are all faith-inclined, and we all choose the object of that faith.

Now, this chapter began with the man's question, "Why is faith such a big deal?" and we've been looking at the importance of faith from several different angles, including a comparison with goodness. And it is true that goodness and faith have been an issue among Christians since the earliest of church times.

In all of his writings the apostle Paul placed a great emphasis on faith. He was fearful those early Christians would come to believe they could be saved through human effort. On the other hand, James in his practical way placed great stress on goodness. "Faith without works is dead," he said. In other words, unless faith produced good actions it was meaningless.

Why Is Faith So Important?

Actually, both Paul and James were right. However, faith is not better that goodness, but faith does precede goodness. There's no chicken-and-egg argument here—our works and our goodness spring from our faith. Our deep-inside, honest-to-God believing determines how we act. If our beliefs are cheap or base, our conduct will be cheap and base. If we fill our minds with things that are superficial, petty, and inconsequential, our actions will reflect the same qualities.

On the other hand, if we fill our souls with that which is good and beautiful, our lives will reflect the good and the beautiful. In the early 1900s a young stage actress spent two years in Europe. Much of this time was spent in concert halls and art museums. Later in life when people asked why she had given so much time to things that were peripheral to her successful career, she answered, "I wanted to expose myself to the best, so I would always know what was better." Perhaps a powerful success factor in her career had been the awareness that her actions, and even her skills, would grow out of her deepest beliefs.

And so we learn that if the Bible seems to emphasize faith over conduct, it is only impressing us with the truth that the "root" comes before the "fruit." It isn't that one is more important than the other; the two are actually inseparable, and there is no conflict between them.

The picture now becomes clear for us as we attempt to live lives obedient to God's purposes—Paul was right; works without faith is dead. James was right; faith without works is dead. This is a powerful, energizing truth that makes a difference in the way we live!

Faith and Love

Up to this point we've looked at "faith" and "goodness." But if you ask the average person what he or she thinks is the most important word in the Christian vocabulary, the answer will most likely be "love." After all, isn't it love that makes the world go around? And didn't the apostle Paul say, "So faith, hope, love abide, these three; but the greatest of these is love"?

And when Jesus was asked what was the greatest commandment, he said that we should love God and our neighbor. Such being the case we might well wonder why that verse in Hebrews 11 doesn't read—"Without *love,* it is impossible to please God."

This leads us to ask, "What is the relationship between faith and love?" The answer to that question parallels the relationship between faith and goodness—faith comes before love. Love becomes possible when we have faith in the value and importance of loving.

Actually, the kind of love pictured in 1 Corinthians 13 demands a tremendous amount of faith. It just isn't natural for us to be patient, kind, unselfish, not irritable, and not concerned primarily with personal gain in all of our relationships—unless we have a profound *belief,* faith, in the value and power of love. This simply means that it is faith which inspires us to love with the intensity Paul calls for in his marvelous "love chapter." On the other hand, this doesn't mean that faith is better than love, but it does precede love, and, in fact, makes love possible.

The Power of Faith

In truth, our lives, our world, are energized by the power of faith—to be truly alive demands faith. This was illustrated for all time by that unique story in the early chapters of Genesis. There Adam and Eve were warned that if they disobeyed God by eating what was forbidden, they would die. And we've already seen that they did disobey and fell under the sentence of death.

But not only were our first parents under the shadow of

Why Is Faith So Important?

physical death at some unknown time in the future, the "death process" became an immediate reality in their lives. For example, it immediately impaired the perfect relationship between Adam and Eve. Before their sin, they had lived together without shame and in complete trust. You remember that Adam referred to Eve as "bone of my bone and flesh of my flesh." They were one. But after their act of unbelief, Adam was quick to blame Eve for what had gone wrong. Now, instead of being "bone of my bone and flesh of my flesh," he referred to her as "the woman you [God] gave me." The beautiful and noble qualities of oneness, trust, and openness had started to fade. Without faith in God these qualities inevitably die.

The same sort of thing happened to Adam and Eve's relationship with the world of nature around them. They were forced to leave their Eden and "till the ground"—to work it "by the sweat of your face." Now nature began to resist their efforts with "thorns and thistles." Because of their lack of faith, something of nature died for them and for their descendants.

In that tragic story we have a vivid and colorful picture of an eternal truth—without faith in God, we die. And I'm not referring only to what we know as eternal death—separation from God. There's also the truth that without faith in God we are not really alive, even though we may be going through the motions of physical life now. Without faith in God and in his goodness we are only partially alive and vast areas of life's potential are dead.

The Phenomenon of Faith

Forty years ago when our nation and most of the civilized world were engulfed in the tragedy of the Second World War, Donald Adams, the book reviewer and literary critic for the *New York Times,* wrote about what he called,

THE POWER OF BELIEVING

"The phenomenon of faith." He wrote that for three years the bestsellers were books based on religious themes. And while they weren't necessarily great books, they reflected the hunger of the times—the desperation of those low moments.

Adams worded his feelings this way: this "revival of faith in *some* form *must* go on. Man cannot live and grow on despair, and no literature can contribute greatly to life, can bring it to that illumination which is its highest service, unless it can find and hold before us values which are positive and constructive."

Despair—lack of faith—closes the door of life. It forces a person's world to become smaller and smaller. Life, love, beauty, and laughter may be all around us, but if we are hunched under an oppressive black cloud of despair, those redemptive qualities of life are shut out—are dead—to us.

By contrast, the faith that Donald Adams spoke of gives life. By faith, we dare to love—and as we love, the boundaries of life are enlarged. By faith, we dare to choose what is right and move ahead boldly into life's struggles. By faith, we are in constant communion with God, but without it we are unaware of his presence and insensitive to his voice.

And while death entered our world when Adam and Eve chose not to believe God, we have life through Christ. Faith in him restores what was lost. The apostle Paul captured this revolutionary truth when he wrote, "I have been crucified with Christ; it is no longer I who live, but Christ who lives in me; and the life I now live in the flesh I live by faith in the Son of God, who loved me and gave himself for me" (Gal. 2:20).

When we have this kind of faith, everything changes—even nature and the world around us. An English preacher friend told me how his world changed after his conversion to Christ. "The next morning the sun was brighter and the birds were singing as I'd never heard them before. And I'd

Why Is Faith So Important?

never seen the grass so green." He had moved back into his Eden. Nothing external had changed, but now he saw the world through faith-lenses. In his description of Saul Kane on the morning after his conversion, John Masefield phrased it beautifully:

> The station brook, to my new eyes,
> Was babbling out of Paradise,
> The waters rushing from the rain
> Were singing Christ has risen again.

When we have the kind of faith Paul wrote about to the Christians in Galatia, something dramatic and exciting happens in all our human relationships. By faith, our friendships take on an intimate and supportive quality. All of our relationships come alive—especially between a husband and wife. When a man and a woman are deeply in love and at peace with God and each other, they have recaptured the spirit of Eden. How often we've heard a couple like that say, "We were meant for each other"—just another way of saying "bone of my bone and flesh of my flesh."

Yes, Adam and Eve lost their Eden by lack of faith. Their world became a nightmare of pain and drudgery. But the Good News for each of us is that by faith in Christ we live again in and through him who is the "pioneer and perfecter of our faith, who for the joy that was set before him endured the cross, despising the shame, and is seated at the right hand of the throne of God" (Heb. 12:2).

We remember Patrick Henry, American Revolutionary War orator and spokesman, for his great "give me liberty or give me death" speech in the old Richmond church. But he gave us an even greater legacy when he said, "My most cherished possession I wish I could leave you is my faith in Jesus Christ, for with him and nothing else you can be happy, but without him and with all else you'll never be happy."

In many instances where faith has succeeded in apparently hopeless circumstances and where it has challenged common sense and logic, the key figure in the story has been a person of ability. And it is true, ability is important—we are to be our best for God. But that isn't the whole story; ability is not enough. In fact, these days ability seems to be in abundant supply and yet so much of what we do is characterized by mediocrity. But as our ability is coupled with the fire of faith in the soul we are inspired to action. It is faith that pushes us out and dares us to reach for the impossible.

{ 4 }

The Faith That Holds On

MANY YEARS AGO, LONG BEFORE TELEVISION, I enjoyed listening to a radio program sponsored by Club Aluminum. It featured familiar hymns sung by George Beverly Shea. This was long before the time of the Billy Graham Crusades and Shea was still a relatively unknown gospel singer.

At the time I didn't know anything at all about Club Aluminum, but I decided that they must be a special kind of a company to put their advertising dollars into a program devoted entirely to gospel music. Back then we didn't have the smorgasbord of religious programming available today, so this type of thing was quite rare. But the hymns were always familiar and Beverly Shea sang them beautifully and with commitment.

Almost thirty years later when I became a member of the Cleveland Rotary Club I was introduced to the "Four-Way Test." More than one million Rotarians in 157 countries accept this Four-Way Test as an ethical guide for business and professional conduct. I hadn't been a Rotarian long before I learned that the Four-Way Test had been written by Mr. Herbert J. Taylor, the Chairman of the Board of Club Aluminum, the very same man who headed the company back in the early days when George Beverly Shea was singing hymns on their program.

The Faith That Holds On

My curiosity was aroused. What kind of a man was this Herbert J. Taylor? Why had he invested thousands of dollars in a hymn-singing program and a little-known singer to advertise his product? What was there about him that gave birth to the Rotarians' Four-Way Test? I set out to find the answer to those questions.

Daring Faith

I hadn't been on my search long before I discovered that Herbert Taylor was not only a highly successful business executive and an outstanding community leader, he was also a man of daring faith. I learned that at the end of World War I he faced the decision which confronts every young man—what he was going to do with his life, the choice of a career.

Young Taylor knew he had a special aptitude for business, but he was also interested in youth work and in the YMCA. While he was wrestling with this decision, he was fortunate in meeting George Perkins, a partner in the J. P. Morgan investment firm. Taylor shared his dilemma with Mr. Perkins, who then gave him some valuable advice—go into business.

"You have a considerable amount of God-given business talent," Perkins said. He predicted that with the passing of time, Taylor would be successful in business and would own his own company. Then he would be able to take time away from that business to finance and pursue youth activities. "By the time you're forty-five," Perkins said, "you'll be spending more of your time on activities to help young people than on your business. And I'll also predict that in later years you'll be working full time with young people."

Herbert Taylor took Mr. Perkins's advice. By the time

he was in his mid-thirties he had become executive vice-president of Jewel Tea, one of America's major food companies. Things were going well and he was being groomed for the presidency of the firm. And because of his ample salary and stock holdings he was financially secure.

Then, in 1932 at the depth of the Great Depression a Chicago bank asked Taylor's senior executive at Jewel Tea if the company would release him half-time to try to rescue nearly bankrupt Club Aluminum Products. Both Taylor and his chief agreed to the arrangement. In a few weeks Taylor learned how badly in debt Club Aluminum was. If just three of its creditors demanded payment, the company would go broke. Not long after that the Creditors' Committee advised Taylor to close out the business, and his senior officer asked him to return full-time with Jewel Tea.

Instead of giving up, though, Taylor relinquished his executive vice-presidency at Jewel Tea and the security it gave him to become the president of Club Aluminum. His salary was one-fifth of what he had been receiving, and he had to borrow $6,000 against his Jewel Tea stock to keep the company afloat. Later he said, "It was quite apparent that I was the only person convinced that the company could be saved." When asked why he was so sure, he responded, "I was convinced because the Holy Spirit told me so."

Now, that is daring language. Some people would even call it irresponsible. But faith sometimes gives people just that kind of daring. And as time passed, Herbert Taylor's dreams came true. His leadership of Club Aluminum saved the company, and he became an extremely wealthy man. While this was happening, Taylor set up a nonprofit organization known as The Christian Workers Foundation. And over the years through his involvement in the Foundation he played a key role in the development of

The Faith That Holds On

Inter-Varsity Christian Fellowship, Young Life, and Child Evangelism Fellowship—all interdenominational youth activities that have greatly affected the lives of millions of young people.

It was during this time, too, that Taylor became the president of the oldest Rotary Club in the world and later assumed the presidency of Rotary International. In both business and Christian service he was a man of bold and daring vision. His daughter recalls a succinct statement Taylor made during those days, "You know, Beverly, there are two kinds of people in this world—those who are led by the Holy Spirit and those who are not."

Daring the Impossible

Through a long and highly successful career Herbert Taylor was motivated by faith that God was leading him. Without a faith that moved him relentlessly to dare the impossible Mr. Taylor might have been just another ordinary business executive. In that case, the Christian organizations which benefited from his faith and vision would never have seen the light of day.

As I reflect on Mr. Taylor's remarkable story, I am reminded again of the story of Abraham. That colorful old patriarch had been comfortably situated in Mesopotamia's "Chicago"—Ur. In Abraham's time Ur was a thriving metropolis, a cultural and business center in the Near East.

At the age of seventy-five Abraham was confronted by God who gave him a rather bizarre set on instructions, "Go from your country and your kindred and your father's house to the land that I will show you . . . ." And next we read, "So Abram went . . ." (Gen. 12:1–6).

THE POWER OF BELIEVING

The New Testament writer of the letter to the Hebrew Christians highlighted the original story by writing, "He [Abraham] went out, not knowing where he was to go." Talk about a daring faith! At seventy-five most of us are settled down firmly in a rocking chair, and when we do venture out on a trip we make sure we know where we're going and even have motel reservations lined up for the whole trip. But Abraham's faith pushed him out to dare the unknown and the seemingly impossible.

George Muller's Faith

A later model of this kind of daring faith is seen in a man named George Muller who with only two shillings in his pocket, established an orphanage in Bristol, England. But then to compound the daring, Muller promised himself and God that he would depend on prayer alone to supply all of the finances. He would never ask for money or let anyone know what his needs were.

Mr. Muller said that if his children ever had to go without a meal he would take it as a sign God didn't want his work to continue. Sometimes they were almost ready to sit down at the table before food arrived, but it always came on time, and, frequently, from unexpected sources.

For sixty years Muller fed his orphans daily, with no one ever missing a meal. Millions of dollars came to George Muller over those years of operating the orphanage. Not once did he ever talk to anyone but God about his needs. Like Abraham—he went out not knowing where he was going.

A still later faith-hero moved into the unknown in a way that many thought was utterly irresponsible. Before Albert Schweitzer was thirty years old he had earned an international reputation as a scholar, theologian, and organist.

The Faith That Holds On

But he turned his back on all this to obtain more training so he could devote his life to being a medical missionary.

If I had been Schweitzer's friend and colleague at that time, I would probably have tried to reason with him something like this, "God has given you a fine mind. Only a handful of people have your intellectual gifts. Stay here and use those gifts. After all, anyone with even limited medical training can do what you're planning to do in Africa." And I suspect that if he had been obstinate and ignored my friendly advice, I'd have said finally, "Schweitzer, you're a fool."

But at thirty-eight he went to Lambarene in the equatorial African jungle and set up his first medical consulting room in a chicken coop. His friends were sure he was burying himself in a senseless effort and that he would probably die an early death in the impossible climate.

From this end of the story, though, we know that just the opposite happened. In a strange way, Schweitzer made Lambarene the center of the world, and in 1952 he was awarded the Nobel Peace prize. And in 1955 Queen Elizabeth II conferred on him the Order of Merit, Great Britain's highest civilian award. During Schweitzer's years at Lambarene, secular and religious leaders made pilgrimages to this African outpost to live on the hospital compound and observe the work being done there. And political leaders arranged interviews with Schweitzer so they could quote him—and, incidentally, to have their pictures taken with him.

Faith and Ability

Now, before leaving our discussion about daring faith and how God uses it, I do want to make a point that I think is most important. Abraham, George Muller, Herbert Taylor, and Albert Schweitzer were all men of ability. They coupled their ability with faith in achieving what they did.

My friend and former parishioner, Hall of Fame quarterback Bart Starr, made me the pleasant butt of a joke in a service club speech several years ago with this story: "Dr. Kalas was playing golf recently with a Catholic friend, Father Joseph Schultz. On each of the first three holes when they got to the green, Father Schultz made the sign of the cross and then sank a long and almost impossible putt.

"After watching this scenario three times Dr. Kalas asked, 'Joe, do you think it would help my putting if I'd make the sign of the cross before approaching the ball?' 'No,' Father Schultz answered. But Dr. Kalas wasn't about to just take no for an answer, so he asked, 'Why not? Because I'm a Protestant?' 'No,' Father Schultz replied, 'because you don't know how to putt.'"

This story is entirely fiction, but it sure went over big that day at the club meeting. But the point of the story is true. In many instances where faith has succeeded in apparently hopeless circumstances and where it has challenged common sense and logic, the key figure in the story has been a person of ability. And it is true, ability is important—we are to be our best for God. That isn't the whole story, however; ability is not enough. In fact, these days ability seems to be in abundant supply and yet so much of what we do is characterized by mediocrity. But as our ability is coupled with the fire of faith in the soul we are inspired to action. It is faith that pushes us out and dares us to reach for the impossible.

Persevering Faith

There's another kind of daring that deserves our attention here, however. We've been speaking of daring and

The Faith That Holds On

dramatic action, and that is important, but it is only part of the story. There is another kind of daring that comes from faith—*a daring that holds on.* This expression of faith may not be as exciting on the surface, but it is the perseverance of faith that in the hard and difficult times of life as well as in the good says, "Let's hold on steady for another day." This is equally daring. In a way, it is this expression of a daring faith that may be more common to most of us.

Earlier, I used Abraham as a model of the faith that dares to venture into the unknown. He is an equally good example of the kind of faith *that holds on.* If Abraham's spirit of daring had depended solely on pumped-up, natural enthusiasm, it might have run dry after two or three years of camping out in the wilderness. But Abraham held on through heat and sandstorms and all kinds of adversity. He held on because as the writer to the Hebrews said, he was looking for that city whose builder and maker is God.

At the same time, though, it is Sarah, Abraham's wife, who models for us a special dimension in understanding the kind of faith *that holds on.* She was one of those wonderful people whose faith has to operate on sort of a *second-hand level.* Now, having worded it that way, I realize there isn't really any such thing as a "second-hand faith." We can't cash in on somebody else's faith, even if that person is a husband or wife or a parent or a pastor. But there may be times when our first-hand faith holds on and is steady because of what someone else has told us or experienced.

As far as we know, that is the way it was with Sarah. There's no hint in the story that God said anything to her about leaving Ur or Haran and going out into the unknown. She took Abraham's word for it and believed because he did. Then, too, it was Abraham who was told he would be the father of many nations. We don't have any record that God told Sarah she would be the mother of many nations. But she believed and accepted that promise because of Abraham.

But then as you will remember from our earlier telling of the story, she did have Isaac. And when Hebrews listed the heroes and heroines of the faith, Sarah is on the list, "By faith Sarah herself received power to conceive, even when she was past the age . . ." (Heb. 11:11). Sarah believed and had faith because Abraham believed and had faith. Both of them had faith to hold steady.

Visionary Faith

So much of God's work in our world is carried on that way—church buildings, schools, hospitals become a reality so often because one person or a small group of persons catch a vision of need and believe that need can be filled. Then others stand behind, and with, those faith-leaders and share in their vision. The faith of the many blends with the faith of the few leaders and together things happen. The faith of thousands of supporters and prayer partners blended with the faith of a Muller or a Schweitzer, with the result that orphan children had a home and the sick were comforted and healed.

I remember one particular father and mother who were in my church. They attended services every Sunday and usually did whatever was asked of them. On the surface there wasn't anything spectacular or daring about them. They were the kind of people who could be counted on, but they always sort of faded into the woodwork.

One day their son told them he felt he had been called to be a missionary. This called for support and preparation

The Faith That Holds On

and ultimately separation. This the parents gave their son gladly even though they had no sense themselves of God's calling. They believed it because their son did; they trusted his faith.

In many ways this kind of faith is as costly and daring as the kind that demands bold and risky action—the kind of faith that acts and accepts a vision or reality that someone else has received. Jesus gave us a graphic illustration of this after his resurrection when Thomas found it impossible to accept the testimony of his fellow disciples and said, "Unless I see in his hands the print of the nails, and place my finger in the mark of the nails, and place my hand in his side, I will not believe" (John 20:25).

The writer of the Gospel of John continues the story by reporting that eight days later, after Thomas had refused to believe, Jesus appeared to the group again and said to Thomas, "Put your finger here, and see my hands; and put out your hand, and place it in my side." It was then that Thomas confessed his belief that Jesus was indeed alive. And it was then, too, that "Jesus said to him, 'Have you believed because you have seen me? *Blessed are those who have not seen and yet believe*'" (John 20:29, italics mine).

Captain Gerald L. Coffee's plane was shot down over Viet Nam in 1966. A prisoner of war for seven years and nine days, he endured solitary confinement for lengthy periods of time. During those years he was allowed to write only twelve six-line postcards to his wife. "Faith was the key to survival," he recalls. And he also remembers how he and the other prisoners developed a tap code so they could send encouraging messages of hope from cell to cell, "Gut it out. I'm praying for you."

Captain Coffee survived those experiences to tell the

story, but biblical faith doesn't offer the promise of deliverance to every prisoner of war. Because in our humanness we somehow admire a faith that "gets results," we pay particular attention to the kind of faith revealed in Captain Coffee's story. That's what we applaud in inspirational magazines and on religious television programs.

After listing the "Hall of Faith" heroes, the writer of the Hebrews "faith chapter" doesn't conclude by saying, "These all came out winners." Instead the writer interrupted himself part way through and wrote, "These all died in faith, not having received what was promised, but having seen it and greeted it from afar" (Heb. 11:13). And then at the very end of the long faith-hero list he wrote, "And all these, though well attested by their faith, *did not receive what was promised* . . ." (Heb. 11:39, italics mine). In other words, they held steady even though they hadn't seen the fulfillment of God's promise and purpose—that takes daring faith!

Optimistic Faith

Robert Louis Stevenson expressed his belief in powerful language, "I believe in an ultimate decency of things; ay, and if I woke in hell, I would still believe it." Stevenson believed so deeply in God and in the rightness of God's universe that he would not allow his own experience, however negatively convincing it might be, to persuade him otherwise. He struggled with illness throughout most of his forty-four years and wrote many of his books from his sickbed. Yet his faith filled him with a divine optimism all the way.

The same kind of "holding-on" faith inspired an unknown man or woman who lived for a time, and perhaps

The Faith That Holds On

died, in a cellar in Cologne. It was one of those dank and fearful holes where Jews hid from the Nazis in World War II. After the war this inscription was found scratched on the wall, "I believe in the sun even when it isn't shining. I believe in love even when I can't feel it. I believe in God even when he is silent." That is a "holding-on" faith!

The apostle Paul had that kind of "holding-on" faith along with the "daring-action" faith that characterized so much of his experience. In spite of the fact that we read frequently about his gift of healing, he wrote these words to his friends in Corinth, ". . . a thorn was given me in the flesh, a messenger of Satan to harass me, to keep me from being too elated. Three times I besought the Lord about this, that it should leave me; but he said to me, 'My grace is sufficient for you, for my power is made perfect in weakness'" (2 Cor. 12:7–9).

It is generally believed this "thorn in the flesh" was a physical ailment that was making Paul's life miserable. Undoubtedly he was able to rationalize that this was a hindrance to his ability to serve God effectively and he should be relieved. But he wasn't, and instead, the Lord reminded him that His grace was enough.

It isn't hard to imagine that someone for whom Paul had prayed could readily have said, "My faith has brought me healing." By contrast in this instance Paul could rightly have said, "My faith has kept me going even when I wasn't healed."

And so we ask, "Is one kind of faith better than the other?" Absolutely not! It is true, of course, in our humanness we'd far prefer a faith that produces healing over a faith that just enables us to hold on. But one is not better than the other. In fact, at times the most daring quality of faith is the one that produces endurance.

THE POWER OF BELIEVING

"Staith"

I like the word "staith." It no longer has a place in our English language, but it's a good word. It rhymes with faith, both in sound and character. It describes the staying quality, the indomitable holding-on, that makes a person stand fast even when the storms of life are raging and he or she feels pressed to the very brink of endurance.

Herbert J. Taylor lived out a daring-action faith when he gave up the security of his executive position at Jewel Tea to become the president of what appeared to be a dying company. But he put that daring into twenty-five words of holding-on faith when he wrote his "Four-Way Test" for Rotarians. And he went on to commit himself and his business to the high ethical standard of the Four-Way Test even when Club Aluminum was still teetering on the edge of bankruptcy.

One day the Club Aluminum people gave a job to a printer because his bid was $500.00 lower than the competing bids. When the job was finished, the printer said that he had made a $500.00 error in his estimate, and he asked if they would be willing to make up the loss. At that time $500.00 was a lot of money, and by contract Club Aluminum had no legal obligation to the printer other than to pay the amount of the bid.

But one of Taylor's associates raised the question of point two in the Four-Way Test: "Is it *fair* to all concerned?" When they checked back over the circumstances related to the bid, they were satisfied that the printer's error was not deliberate, so they paid him the amount of the original bid plus $500.00. I believe Taylor and his associates exhibited true "staith"—that quality of faith described by Augustine, "Understanding is the reward of faith. Therefore, seek not to

The Faith That Holds On

understand that thou mayest believe, but believe that thou mayest understand."

When We Ask Why?

We Americans especially find it difficult to appreciate this holding-on kind of faith. It isn't that we lack the ability to persist, but we are completely success-oriented. We believe that if we follow the rules, we ought to get the right results. And then when things don't turn out the way we expect them to, we get all bogged down in "Why?" Why wasn't my friend healed when he was such a wonderful Christian and we were all praying for him? Why didn't my business succeed when I was so sure the Lord led me into it and was guiding me each step of the way? Why? . . . Why?

When it comes right down to the nitty-gritty of things, the question "Why?" is completely irrelevant under the umbrella of faith. This is not to say that in our humanness we won't ask it. And it is possible that asking why isn't always an exercise in futility—the mere asking may at times help us to gain better insight. But faith's final attitude has to be—"It doesn't matter whether or not my prayer is answered in the way I might want and expect. Actually, my faith is not in my prayers and it isn't in the results I get. My faith is in *God*—nothing else."

In July of 1967 Joni Eareckson was a beautiful, bright, athletic girl. She had graduated from high school only a few weeks before. In high school she had been a member of the National Honor Society and was the captain of her lacrosse team. Joni was looking forward to attending college in the fall and to running her horse in summer competition at the shows.

THE POWER OF BELIEVING

In the late afternoon of July 30 she dove into the waters of Chesapeake Bay as she had done so often before. But this time her calculation was inches off and her head struck a hard surface. As a result she was paralyzed from the shoulders down.

For weeks Joni hovered between life and death, and she was terrified by the deepening realization that most of her body would always be dead. At age seventeen, there seemed little hope for her future. There were moments when she thought only of suicide, but in the indignity of her helplessness she couldn't have carried through even if she had really wanted to.

The on-going sequel of her story is now well known through her several books, the movie of her life, and her testimony on televised Billy Graham Crusades. She's an artist who has become very proficient in holding her brush between her teeth. And her testimony in word and song has made a profound difference in many people.

I'm sure that many have prayed and continue to pray that Joni will be healed. And maybe she will be. We certainly can't put boundaries around God's will and purposes. But of one thing we can be sure: if someday on this earth Joni walks again, the faith that will permit her to do so is no better than the faith that sustains her every day now in her wheelchair—the faith that keeps her laughing and rejoicing in the Lord, even in the midst of her difficulties.

The poet Browning wrote that our reach should exceed our grasp, "or what's a heaven for?" Faith inspires us to reach beyond our grasp, to do daring things. Faith may lead us into places and situations that logic says are quite impossible, like Abraham moving out into the unknown or Schweitzer leaving the comfortable world of music and theological inquiry to build a hospital in the African jungle. There may even be times when faith reaches for accomplishments that it cannot grasp. But even then it loses none of its integrity in the process.

The Faith of Captain Scott

In 1935 a memorial was dedicated in England to Captain Robert Falcon Scott. This memorial is actually the first Polar museum in the world. Across the front of the building is a Latin inscription intended to describe Scott. It reads, "He sought the secrets of the Pole. He found the secrets of God."

The story behind the inscription is one of the most heroic in human history. While still in his early thirties Captain Scott set out in 1910 to reach the South Pole. He and his little crew set sail from New Zealand and immediately began to encounter serious and unexpected difficulties. Eventually, however, they set up headquarters at Cape Evans on Ross Island.

Moving out from Ross Island in November of 1911, the party of five began the trek over the ice with sledges. At first they used hardy little ponies that had been trained on the tundras of Siberia, but the animals floundered in the powdery snow and eventually their legs were broken when they fell into hidden crevasses. Their dogs, huskies from the Yukon, fared little better.

Finally, in desperation Scott and his four companions harnessed themselves to a sledge that weighed a thousand pounds and struggled on. At 9,000 feet above sea level, on rough ice, and in frigid air, their task seemed impossible. But they were fiercely brave men, and they had a unique goal—to be the first human beings to reach the South Pole.

On the fourteenth day of their inhuman struggle they reached the Pole only to find a tattered flag of Norway fluttering in the cold and silence. Roald Amundsen, the Norwegian explorer, had reached the Pole only a month before. After years of preparation and months of struggle Scott and his party had to be satisfied with second place.

The worst of their tragedy was yet to come. The five men started back to their base camp in weather that seemed committed to their destruction. The strongest man in the group, Petty Officer Evans, died from a bad fall on the ice. Next Captain Oates suffered such severe frostbite that he was badly crippled. He realized that because of his condition he was slowing down his companions. One night Oates walked out from the camp alone in a blinding blizzard to die, so he would no longer imperil the others.

But Scott and the other two struggled on. On February 19, 1912, fifty days after they had left the Pole, they set up camp for the last time. Their diaries indicated that at the time they had just enough fuel to make two cups of tea apiece and enough food to keep them alive for two days. According to their calculations they were only eleven miles from their base camp. They felt that with one final burst of effort they could make it.

Instead, that night a blizzard closed in on them making it impossible for them to press on. They knew they were lost. Before he died Captain Scott wrote a letter to Sir James Barrie describing their last moments. Among other things, he wrote, "It would do your heart good if you could hear us fill our tent with ringing songs of cheer."

Those brave men lost in their race to the South Pole, and they died alone out there on the ice. Their frozen bodies, along with their diaries, records, and letters, were found eight months later. But they died as winners. By faith, they sought the secrets of the South Pole, and by faith they found the secrets of God. Theirs was a never-to-be-forgotten faith that dared to move out into the unknown, and from the unknown they dared to hold on to the end.

Faith That Made a Difference

When my wife Ruth and I moved to Watertown, Wisconsin, in the fall of 1950, we discovered that in this city of 13,000 there was only one black family. That family, the Goodlettes, belonged to our little congregation. They were a professional music group known as "The Goodie Family," and had settled down in Watertown a year or so before we arrived.

I hadn't been at the church long before I became acquainted with Walter Goodlette and learned some of his family background. It seems they had traveled for years as "good will ambassadors between the races." But now they felt it was time for them to settle down in one place and prove their convictions about race relations by living side-by-side with white families. They had deliberately chosen Watertown because there were no other black families in the community.

When they had arrived in town, they attempted immediately to buy property, but that wasn't easy. At the time there were no laws to protect them, but this didn't concern Walter because he knew that resorting to legal means would not create a friendly situation. After a time an independent-minded woman sold them a modest house but at an asking price well above its market value. "Mr. Goodie," as most of us knew him, was hurt and disappointed, but he paid the asking price without becoming embittered.

At one point during our stay in Watertown we were

temporarily without a choir director. And while Walter's specialty was not choir directing, he was the most qualified person to fill our immediate need, so I asked him if he would help us out on a temporary basis. He said he'd be willing to do that but only if the choir itself discussed privately how they felt about having a black leader.

When I conveyed Walter's request to the choir, they looked honestly perplexed for a moment. Then Bill Urban spoke up, "I have to stop and think what color Mr. Goodie is. He's not a black man or a white man; he's just Walter Goodlette." That settled it once and for all.

As the years passed, the Goodlette children left the community for college and jobs. This left Walter and his wife alone. Eventually, they closed their little business and went into retirement. But they had been a model of indomitable will and faith. They had believed they could make a difference in Watertown, and they did. Walter and his family had entered a daring faith venture when they moved to Watertown in 1949. They had risked possible physical harm and rejection. But they had a faith that "held on"—that persevered.

Patient Faith

In the nineteenth century George MacDonald, after failing as a parish minister—the ultimate humiliation in his Scottish culture—became a writer. For years he wrote with only modest success. But finally, his skill as a writer of fantasies, children's stories, and sublime poetry won him acclaim and he became one of the best-known and most-loved English writers of his time. It was one of MacDonald's books that gave C. S. Lewis his first nudge toward Christianity. Lewis said of him, "I know hardly any other writer who seems closer, or more continually close, to the Spirit of Christ himself."

MacDonald himself once said, "The principal part of faith is patience." Out of the pain of his own personal experience he knew and understood the holding-on quality of daring faith. It was this faith that gave him (and gives us) the divine audacity to dare and the courage to hold on.

It has seemed to me at times that I've known people who had a bigger gift of faith than I have. But then I have to ask myself whether God shows favorites— does he give a bigger gift of faith to some other person than he gives me? And my answer to that question is, "No, I don't think so." This then leads me to feeling that the Lord gives us faith as a gift, *but we choose how we'll use it*. In other words, it's what we do with what we have that makes the difference.

5

Faith That Moves Mountains

THE MODERN-DAY SONG WRITER RAY HILDEBRAND wrote some lovely lyrics centering around the idea expressed by Jesus about a faith that moves mountains. But then he gives the whole idea a unique twist when he suggests that the mountain which needs to be moved "is me."

As I have reflected on those words, I've decided that most of us would probably agree with Ray Hildebrand. Because of our teaching and religious background it is likely most of us would accept as valid the words of Jesus when he promised that faith no larger than a mustard seed had the power to move "mountains." But when it comes right down to the nitty-gritty of everyday living, to the "mountain" of our own feelings—our drives and our deepest desires—a feeling haunts most of us that we just don't have enough faith.

It's true, of course, that in our thoughtful moments we know there is no way we can even get up in the morning without having a kind of faith. But we also know there's a big difference between what we have and the daring, risk-taking kind of faith that some of our biblical ancestors had. And there's a notable difference between the kind of faith such persons as Muller and Schweitzer had and that a person like

Mother Teresa has as she ministers to India's sick and dying—and what we have.

As we've already come to understand, all of us have sort of a native faith-capacity engineered into us. Now, though, we want to explore just how we obtain a faith that not only moves mountains of difficulties out of the way but reaches out to other "mountains" in a creative and redemptive way—a faith centered on God and his purposes for all of life.

Faith Defined

From the first verse of Genesis to the last verse of Revelation the Bible is, of course, a faith document. Yet, surprisingly, it tells us almost nothing about how to get a God-centered faith. In fact, it doesn't spend much time defining faith in a pragmatic and precise way. The clearest definition we have is given to us by the writer of the letter to the Hebrews, "Now faith is the assurance of things hoped for, the conviction of things not seen" (11:1). But those somewhat poetic words most likely fall short of satisfying the practical person who wants specific steps or rules. Most of the time our Bible shows us faith in action and leaves definitions and interpretations up to us. There's no neatly packaged set of instructions. And even when we look at the lives of those faith-heroes in our Bible in terms of piety and style we don't come away with "four easy steps to daring faith."

There was a time in our history when faith in God seemed to be a more natural part of the human condition. Historian Will Durant classified the period from Constantine to Dante—roughly from the fourth through the thirteenth centuries—as the "age of faith." On the surface, at least, during that period of time the masses of people in the

Western world seemed more inclined to believe in God rather than doubt him.

But in the early days of the twentieth century Henry Van Dyke, the preacher-poet, described that time as "the age of doubt." And in spite of those occasional moments of spiritual awakening that have occurred in our century, Van Dyke's label might well apply to our present time. At least these have not been years that could be described as a time of great faith.

Noah's Faith

But the twentieth century faith-mood shouldn't discourage us. Some of the Bible's great faith personalities lived in times hostile to faith in God. In the gripping story of Noah the Genesis writer tells us that "The Lord saw that the wickedness of man was great in the earth, and that *every imagination of the thoughts of his heart was only evil continually*" (Gen. 6:5, italics mine). From this we see that Noah lived in some pretty desperate days. It was a time of such violence and corruption that God decided to wipe out the whole mess and start over.

In spite of those evil conditions we read that "Noah was a righteous man, blameless in his generation." Noah was not a victim of the corrupt society that surrounded him. Instead he managed to rise above his hostile environment. Most certainly, Noah did not live in an "age of faith," but he was a man of faith.

The Faith of Moses

Another great faith-personality among our biblical ancestors was Moses. For Moses, the conditions were very different from those that plagued Noah. Because of the unique circumstances that followed his birth, Moses grew up in the ease and luxury of Pharaoh's palace. It would have been easy for him to be lulled into an apathetic acceptance of the status quo. He could easily have been victimized by a life of plenty. But the writer of Hebrews writes that "when he was grown up, [he] refused to be called the son of Pharaoh's daughter, choosing rather to share ill-treatment with the people of God than to enjoy the fleeting pleasures of sin" (Heb. 11:24–25). For Moses, the ease of palace life was hostile to faith in God, but he was a man of faith anyway.

And, yes, while I refuse to be a member of the doom-and-gloom crowd today, there is much about the mood of our world that is not the best for developing and nurturing a solid faith in God. The distractions of our electronic and space age may not necessarily be hostile to faith in God but neither are they particularly conducive to faith.

Faith Is Irrepressible

The great Good News for us, however, is that faith prospers even under the most difficult of circumstances. It isn't like a delicate flower that depends on a controlled, hothouse environment. Instead, faith can better be compared to a hardy green shoot that forces its way through a crack in the rocks or a crack in an asphalt parking lot. In reality, with nature, daring faith is irrepressible.

Thus we come back to the question, "How do we acquire faith and what are we to do to help that faith grow and mature?" How do we acquire a faith that works and holds steady in the best of times as well as in the worst of times?

The Source of Faith

Fortunately, the apostle Paul speaks directly to the question of where faith comes from. In writing to the Christians at Rome, Paul says, "So faith comes from what is heard, and what is heard comes by the preaching of Christ" (Rom. 10:17). The first thing Paul is telling his readers here is that faith comes from something we hear. This ties in with a modern theory of education—"Whatever gets your attention, gets you." We become what we hear.

In a way, that is a frightening truth. Probably no generation in history up to this point has "heard" as much as we do. I read a comment recently that said the average person reads between 10,000 and 20,000 words a day—magazines, newspapers, letters, billboards, books, cereal boxes, and so on. In addition we "hear" at least another 20,000 words—conversation, radio, television, tapes, and so on. We are bombarded with words—voices and ideas.

The words we hear make a profound impression on us. You remember as children we used to chant the little ditty, "Sticks and stones will break my bones, but words will never hurt me." Don't you believe it!

The Sounds of Negativism

It is hard to escape the words and sounds of negativism. Many of us are awakened each morning by a clock radio that is set on a newscast. That is almost a sure downer. I've heard it said that newspeople have a "vested interested in disaster." The six o'clock television news features homicides, fires, accidents, threat of war and nuclear disaster, famine in Third World countries, and name-calling between heads of government. We hear accounts of rape, child abuse and molestation, federal and state officials convicted of income tax crimes and perjury, of broken marriages, and of babies being born to twelve-year-old mothers.

I used to escape this sort of thing by reading the sports pages. But now these are filled with bad news—drug abuse and death, contract disputes, and athletes holding out on valid contracts because management won't increase their annual take from $250,000 to a half-million dollars.

Now, I haven't rehearsed all of this to drive you down into the dumps of despair. Quite the opposite. But part of the solution to any problem is to acknowledge the way conditions are and then go on. As Christians we aren't to give in to the negativism and bad faith loose in our world. Instead, we are to stand tall and "hear" the words of positive faith.

A Georgia mother, Becky Cooper, learned to do this. Todd, her two-year-old son, suffered what the doctors called "irreparable brain damage" in a near-drowning accident. Becky and her husband watched over Todd's bed for three months before he even so much as wiggled a toe. And their vigil lasted another three months before he came out of the coma.

During those months of struggle they learned that some visitors to Todd's room radiated an optimistic faith. Others cast a pall of despair and gloom over the room. Becky recalls, "Staying upbeat was so important that I even put a sign on Todd's door that read, 'Everything said here must be *positive.*'" That's a sign that most of us could hang on our door. This doesn't mean that we wander through life ignoring facts, but at the same time we must always bear in mind that possibly we haven't heard *all* of the facts—perhaps we haven't really heard from God!

I think it is terribly important for us to take seriously Paul's words, "Faith comes from what is heard." We can control what we really "hear." This is why it is so tragic when we let ourselves get into the awful ruts of being negative and seeing only the dark side of life. The German philosopher Goethe once said, "I will listen to anyone's convictions, but pray keep your doubts to yourself."

THE POWER OF BELIEVING

The sure sign of a person without a daring faith is a negative attitude—such people worry and always see the dark side of life. Their very presence casts a shadow upon everyone around them. I remember a minister friend of mine who frequently began his sentences this way, "I don't want to be negative, but . . . ." It was for this kind of a person that Becky Cooper put her sign on Todd's door. "Yes, but . . ." is a deadly infection that can pollute any social atmosphere and smother faith.

"Pray and Let God Worry"

I've always enjoyed this charming little story about Martin Luther. He dearly loved his wife Katie and was devoted to her, but it seems he had to struggle all the time with her dreadful habit of worry. Once when he was traveling, he wrote her this letter, "To the saintly, worrying Lady Katherine Luther, doctor at Zulsdorf and Wittenberg, my gracious, dear wife. We thank you heartily for being so worried that you can't sleep, for since you started worrying about us, a fire broke out near my door, and yesterday, no doubt due to your worry, a big stone, save for the dear angels, would have fallen and crushed us like a mouse in a trap. If you don't stop worrying, I'm afraid the earth will swallow us. Pray and let God worry. Cast your burden on the Lord."

That beautiful tongue-in-cheek letter not only tells us a lot about Katherine Luther, but we learn a great deal about the old reformer himself. What a delightful sense of humor! I just have to believe that kind of an attitude is a true reflection of God-given faith—and love.

Friends and Faith

"Faith comes from what is heard." A most important way to control what we hear and to nurture and build our faith lies, I believe, in the careful selection of friends who have a positive faith. I know that I was greatly strengthened in my own faith even during my high school years by several friends. From them I "heard" words that bolstered my own faith as we shared our experiences. We affirmed each other in a positive way.

Henry Sloane Coffin, for many years the senior minister at Madison Avenue Presbyterian Church in New York, in the style of his times, captured the importance of Christian friends when he wrote, "You and I cannot expect a satisfactory intercourse with the Invisible save as we keep company with men and women who are very sure of God." That is our birthright as Christians—there will most certainly be a lot in life that we don't understand, but we can be *very sure of God*.

My own life is greatly enriched by being with certain people. When we're together—either one-on-one or in a group—I "hear" wholesome, affirming, faith-filled words. Of course we talk about our struggles, our hopes, and our dreams. We share our disappointments, our failures, and our successes. We share with each other those times when we've fallen flat on our faces as well as those moments of victory when it seemed we could actually feel God's presence. But whether we're up or down we try to use words that affirm our innermost belief in God. Even in our hard times we try to remember, as the prophet Elisha was reminded, that "those who are with us are more than those that are with them."

Faith-Building Books

I read about a young ministerial student who complained to his father that he was disappointed in his seminary professors. His father, a very wise man, didn't commiserate with him about his teachers, but merely said,

THE POWER OF BELIEVING

"Son, learn as much as you can from the 50,000 teachers in the library."

Reading faith-building books and making friends of their authors is a powerful means of nurturing our belief in God. As we fill our minds and hearts with the powerful words of our Christian faith, we're storing up truth that can slowly and steadily move us toward deeper and richer experiences with God.

One day when I was visiting in a nursing home, someone told me about a lady who listened faithfully to the Sunday broadcast of our church service. I had a delightful visit with her. In fact, being with this new friend gave me a lift that day. Early in our conversation she explained that she was blind but that early in life she had committed to memory the words of dozens of hymns. Then she added, "They help me now. I sing them to myself, and they always give me a lift." She had made friends of those hymnwriters through their words, and now, even though she couldn't see the pages of her hymnbook, the words of her old "friends" continued to enrich her life.

But while friends, books, and music can do much to build our faith, nothing is more significant than the words we hear when we meet with other believers in the worship service of the church. Yes, Paul has written that "faith comes from what is heard," but then he goes on to write that "what is heard comes by the preaching of Christ" (Rom. 10:17b). It is the preaching, the teaching, the witnessing to the Good News of life in Christ that counts. And when people "hear" that Good News, life takes on an altogether different dimension.

Unfortunately, though, a great deal of our preaching, teaching, and witnessing takes on a tone that is so much a part of our news today. Negative, angry sounding, and accusative preaching and witnessing don't inspire faith. If we base our witness on what is bad, we're driven to feelings of despair and hopelessness.

God Isn't Dead

In the early 1800s Frederick Douglass, the runaway slave, stirred New England audiences with his powerful speeches against the evil of slavery. But one night in Boston his speech took on a despairing tone. On this particular occasion, after speaking boldly on the evils of slavery, he expressed his feeling that the situation was hopeless, that the white people of America would never end the black man's bondage short of an armed revolt. Then he went on to admit that such a revolt would produce wholesale slaughter. It was a grim picture and one could almost feel the thickness of the cloud of pessimism and despair that filled the room.

Then a gaunt, poorly dressed black woman stood up and in a deep voice she shouted, "Frederick, is God dead?" As a rule Douglass had a ready response to hecklers, but this time he stood in silence—a silence shattered in a few moments as the audience broke into thunderous applause.

No, even though we may act as if He is at times, "God isn't dead." And it is important that we sound and look and act like he isn't—not just once in a while but all of the time. One of the best ways I know to set the stage for this kind of an attitude is to begin each day in the mood of the psalmist when he wrote, "This is the day which the Lord has made; let us *rejoice* and be glad in it" (Ps. 118:24, italics mine).

Sometimes on Sunday morning when I look around at the long faces of people sitting in church I wonder what the Lord must think about it all. Worship is to be a celebration of faith, and we are supposed to look like we're celebrating. I recall once being in a service when the clergyman opened with the words, "I was glad when they said unto me, let us go into the house of the Lord." Unfortunately, he looked as pained as if he were making an appearance in traffic court.

One of the most delightful and provocative humorists on today's scene is Erma Bombeck. In one of her columns she told about the little boy who was sitting in front of her in church. He was just as quiet as could be and certainly wasn't bothering anyone, but every once in a while he would turn around and smile happily at everyone behind him. He did this several times to the pleasure of everyone who could see him. Suddenly his mother jerked him around and told him in a loud whisper to stop grinning—he was in church. Then when the tears came to the little fellow's eyes, his mother said, "That's better." I could identify with Erma Bombeck's reaction when she said that she would liked to have given the boy a big hug and told him about her happy, smiling God.

Sing and Celebrate

There are powerful faith-building possibilities for all of us as we come together with our fellow Christians in the teaching and worshiping climate of the church. But such moments are meant to be great times of joy and celebration. In our profound moments of learning and worship, what is "heard" is the magnificent poetry of our hymns, the inspiring words of prayer and Scripture, the Word of God that "comes by the preaching of Christ," and the words of our Christian friends—fellow strugglers—as they share with us their own pilgrimage of faith.

A little further on in Paul's letter to his Christian friends in Rome he prayed a prayer for them that we would do well to make ours when we come together in worship:

"May the God of hope fill you with all joy and peace in believing, so that by the power of the Holy Spirit you may abound in hope" (Rom. 15:13). These words, when "heard" with ears of faith, build faith—a "hallelujah" faith that is full of the authentic joy of the Lord.

There is another source for the words we "hear" that deserves our attention, and on the surface it may seem a bit strange at first. But the words we hear from our self-talk carry powerful and life-changing potential. Our wonderful Lord has engineered into each of us an amazing mechanism—our minds. If we choose to think negative and gloomy thoughts, our whole attitude toward life and our faith will be negative and gloomy. On the other hand if we flood our minds with faith-thoughts and the joy of the Lord is our strength (Neh. 8:10), we can "say to this mountain [ourselves], 'Move from here to there,' and it will move; and nothing will be impossible to you" (Matt. 17:21).

One of John Bunyan's characters in *Pilgrim's Progress* is Mr. Facing Both Ways, a man of no firm faith—unable to choose a direction and move forward with determination. The writer of the letter of James described this character well when he spoke of the "double-minded man [who is] unstable in all his ways." And he further refers to one who doubts—lacks faith—as being like "a wave of the sea . . . driven and tossed by the wind" (James 1:6–8).

Full of Faith

On the other hand, another of Bunyan's characters is Mr. Steadfast. His mind was full of faith; he knew where he was going. And while Bunyan doesn't say so, I have to believe that Mr. Steadfast filled his mind with positive faith-words of joy and confidence in the Lord.

THE POWER OF BELIEVING

When I was a teenager a friend gave me some advice that I've never forgotten, "Believe your beliefs and doubt your doubts." It was sometime later, though, that I came to understand that *we choose* whether to believe or doubt. We choose whether to exercise faith so that our "mountain" is moved. And powerful factors in that choosing process are the words we "hear" which we ourselves have fed into the vast storehouse of our mind.

Martin Luther would sometimes repeat over and over again, "I am baptized. I am baptized." By setting his mind firmly on the central fact of his faith in Christ as symbolized by baptism Luther was able to stand firmly against the doubts that plagued him. One of the most powerful affirmations in all of Scripture comes toward the end of Paul's letter to his friends at Philippi, "I *can do all things* in him who strengthens me" (Phil. 4:13, italics mine). That is a marvelous "day opener." As we flood our minds with that positive expression of faith, our faith will grow and mature, and we will become Mr. or Mrs. or Miss Steadfast!

There are two other pictures which describe faith in our New Testament that give us some insight on how to obtain and nurture it. First, we come to understand that it is a *gift* of the Spirit. And the second picture is this: faith is a *fruit* of the Spirit. It is true, of course, that no picture is complete and perfect in every detail. These descriptions of faith do give us helpful insight, however, into something that is indeed difficult to understand.

Faith is a gift. It is part of the bounty God has showered on us so generously. Now, in its generic form faith is something everyone has—the kind that causes us to get up in the morning. This kind of faith moves us out to take a chance on eating and drinking and working; it gives us the courage to marry and have families and establish friendships.

But the kind of faith we're talking about here—faith in

Faith That Moves Mountains

God, a faith that although as tiny as a mustard seed can help us move our mountains of difficulty . . . a faith that is described as "being sure of what we hope for and certain of what we do not see." That is most certainly a gift—from God.

It has seemed to me at times that I've known people who had a bigger gift of faith than I have. But then I have to ask myself whether God shows favoritism—does he give a bigger gift of faith to some other person than he gives me? And my answer to that question is, "No, I don't think so." This then leads me to feel that the Lord gives us faith as a gift, *but we choose how we'll use it.* In other words, it's what we do with what we have that makes the difference.

This idea can be illustrated in sort of a homely way by certain great athletes whose physical equipment wasn't necessarily the greatest, but they excelled in spite of their drawbacks. For example, during his years with the Baltimore Colts Raymond Berry was one of the greatest pass receivers in all of professional football. But Ray wasn't especially large or a particularly fast runner. He was near-sighted and suffered with back problems, but in spite of all that he was one of the best offensive ends of all time. He used the athletic gifts he had. He practiced and believed in himself. And he became the gifted coach of the New England Patriots professional football team.

I take great comfort in the fact that all of the great faith-heroes mentioned in Hebrews 11 were ordinary people just like we are. They were intensely human. For example, Moses really bungled things by losing his temper and killing the Egyptian slavemaster. At that moment I doubt that anyone would have considered him a man of faith. And then, even after forty years of herding sheep in the Sinai desert where he had plenty of time to reflect, he still hadn't learned to fully trust and believe God. After meeting the Lord in the burning bush, he still argued with God, claiming not to be qualified for the mission assigned to him. Here, too, he didn't earn any blue ribbons for his faith. But over the long haul, he earned his place in the Hall of Faith.

As a matter of fact, the parade of faith-heroes that has marched across the centuries from the time of Jesus—Peter and Paul, Augustine, Francis of Assisi, Martin Luther, John Knox, John Wesley, Roger Williams, Dietrich Bonhoeffer—have all been people who struggled with their faith, but they persevered. They coveted "earnestly the best gift." Or as a later translation puts it, they were people who ". . . eagerly desire the greater gifts" (1 Cor. 12:31 NIV). The gifts of God, including faith, come to those who "covet earnestly," who "eagerly desire" them. Yes, earth-moving faith is a gift; we can't earn it. But by our desire, we can receive and nurture the gift.

Faith is a fruit of the Spirit. We are most certainly not creators who can produce fruit out of nothing, but we can do a great deal to prepare the environment and soil of our lives so conditions are right for the "fruit" to grow. We can nurture our life-plant and prune our life-tree and greatly improve the quality of our life-fruit. By study, prayer, Christian fellowship, we can cultivate an enlarged capacity for great faith, a faith that carries us through the routines of family and vocation as well as through life's most intense struggles.

Somewhere I read about the music lover who was visiting New York City and wanted to see the famed Carnegie Hall. After getting rather fuzzy directions and walking for a time, he was quite sure he was in the neighborhood, but he hadn't been able to spot the building itself. Suddenly, across the street he saw a young man carrying a violin case and hustling along as if he knew exactly where he was going.

Faith That Moves Mountains

Hurrying across the street while dodging traffic, the music lover approached the young musician and asked, "Pardon me, but can you tell me how to get to Carnegie Hall?" Without a moment's hesitation the young violinist responded, "Practice, man, practice."

Somehow or other, without stretching the analogy too far, I think I can imagine our loving Lord responding to the question about how we get a stronger faith by saying "Practice, friend, practice—use what you've got."

A pastor told his congregation one Sunday, "I read the fourteenth chapter of St. John's Gospel the other day, and as I did so, I saw my Lord's face shine through the printed page, and the world stood still." That is the vision God intends for each of us to have. It is a faith-vision that focuses on God's life-changing, world-changing power. If we see it, we can have it. God wills it so.

{ 6 }

If You See It You Can Have It!

When the great, blind Scottish preacher, George Matheson, became pastor of St. Bernard's Church in Edinburgh, there was an old woman in the congregation who lived in a cellar. Her living conditions were miserable, but apparently she took the filth and gloom for granted. She had lived that way for so long that the ugly disarray seemed normal.

After Matheson had been at the church for several months, it came time for the celebration of the Lord's Supper. In the style of the Scottish church, an elder called to see if the woman wanted a communion card to admit her to the Lord's Table. He found that she had moved from the basement, and eventually he traced her to an attic room. She was as poor as ever, so the furnishings in her garret were plain and simple. But the attic was light, clean, and airy in dramatic contrast to the dirty basement where she had previously lived. "I see you've changed your house," the elder said to the old woman. "Ay," she said, "I have. You canna hear George Matheson preach and live in a cellar."

There's too much cellar living in our world. It has nothing to do with money or education; many who are generously endowed with one or both of these blessings are still living far below God's intention and their own divine potential. Unfortunately, even a good many Christian people live as if God were dead or at least as if He had forsaken them. But this old Scottish woman had discovered an important truth: when a new vision comes to us, all of life's perspectives are changed. We may be content to live in a cellar if that's all of life we know. But when some person or some experience helps us to see that life has its sunlight and its higher rooms, we have to move out of the basement.

Years ago a friend gave me a phrase that I turn to again and again: *If you see it, you can have it.* Unfortunately, our lives are small because our vision is limited.

Juan Vazquez is the senior member of "The Flying Vazquez," the only aerial team that has ever accomplished the quad, a dazzling flight through the air that includes four somersaults. His team is now able to succeed with the quad about 35 percent of the time. But Juan plans to bring the level of success up to 70 percent. He says, "It's a tough goal, but I remember these words, 'What your mind can conceive, you can do.'"

Beyond Ourselves

Much secular self-help literature emphasizes this theme. And that's all right as far as it goes, but I want to go further. Normal human enthusiasm is good for as long as the circumstances are encouraging or until our emotional tank runs dry, but when that time comes, most of us chug slowly to a halt. We need a resource beyond ourselves. It is not only a matter of seeing what a grand dream we'd like to have fulfilled, nor of realizing our own gifts for bringing our dreams to pass, but of knowing that God has unlimited resources, and that his attitude toward us is generous beyond measure.

Juan Vazquez says in a *Guideposts* magazine article that his dreams have a more substantial base than unaided human ambition. He was inspired to accept in faith the words of Jesus that if we pray for something and believe that we will receive it, we will.

Juan and his aerial family cooperated with God and their own convictions. They didn't sit and wait for achievement to come to them; they practiced literally thousands of hours. And they were stimulated to practice tirelessly because they had received a vision of what they could do.

It is the vision of our potential under God and his generosity toward us that compels us to keep trying. If it weren't for this, we might give up, especially when our efforts meet with defeat or when we're simply weary or disenchanted with the struggle. It is so important at such times to have a grand vision of the possibilities—to believe that "if you see it, you can have it."

Opening Our Inward Eyes

The apostle Paul phrased this idea so eloquently in his letter to his friends in Ephesus when he prayed that their inward eyes might be illumined so they could clearly picture the hope to which God had called them. And he further urged them to see the wealth of God's glory and the vast resources of his power that was theirs in Christ (Eph. 1:18, 19).

This is one of those times when Paul seems to overflow with the excitement of what he wants to say as his words tumble out in one grand phrase after another. It is almost as if he can't wait to tell his readers the good news. He wants his fellow believers to have their "inward eyes . . . illumined" so they can see the richness God has provided. And if they see it—if their inward eyes can catch the vision—they can have it.

But what keeps us from catching the vision? The answer to that question begins to come clear in a moving story found in 2 Kings. Here we read that the prophet Elisha and his servant were trapped in a city surrounded by an enemy army. In panic, the servant asked the prophet what they were going to do—the situation looked absolutely hopeless. But Elisha answered calmly, "Don't be afraid, the army protecting us is larger than our attackers." And having said that, Elisha prayed, "Lord, open up his eyes that he may see." Then, wonder of wonders, through his newly "opened" eyes the servant discovered that the surrounding mountains were alive with the chariots of God.

Most of us are just like Elisha's servant. We become so absorbed with the easily visible armies of despair that we simply don't see all the forces working for us and cheering us on. But if we would stop now and then to take an inventory of our resources—to count our blessings—the Lord would "open our eyes" too. There's an army on our side. And while the forces with us may not be as clearly seen as our opposition, if we will look beyond our immediate desperation, we, too, can see the forces of God at work in our world.

But that is what faith is all about! Adam and Eve got in trouble because they were more impressed with the immediate possibilities of the forbidden fruit than they were with the long-range promise of God. Moses, says the writer of Hebrews, had to look beyond the clamoring pleasures of Pharaoh's palace and "look off toward the reward."

Living in the Real World

Cyprian, the third-century Christian martyr, analyzed the differences in our vision in a letter to Donatus. Cyprian said that the world might look very cheerful from a sheltered garden. "But if I were to ascend some high mountain and look out over the wide lands, you know very well what I should see: brigands on the highways, pirates on the sea, armies fighting, cities burning; in the amphitheaters men murdered to please applauding crowds; selfishness and cruelty and misery and despair under all roofs. It is a bad world, Donatus, an incredibly bad world. But I have discovered in the midst of it a quiet and holy people who have learned a great secret. They have found a joy which is a thousand times better than any pleasure of our sinful life. They are despised and persecuted, but they care not. They are masters of their souls. They have overcome the world. These people, Donatus, are the Christians—and I am one of them."

Cyprian's words are especially insightful. He notes, on the one hand, that a person can so isolate himself or herself from the troubles of life—living in a kind of dream world—that everything will seem beautiful. Obviously, this is an irresponsible way to live. By contrast, though, there is the real world—one threatened by violence, selfishness, cruelty, and despair.

As I read Cyprian's words, I'm impressed by how easily they could be descriptive of our own times, for we, too, live in a world of violence and crime. But while Cyprian didn't close his eyes to the violence of his times, neither did his vision stop there. He knew he was among those who had overcome the world.

Where Is Our Faith Focused?

Unfortunately, though, it is possible for our vision to become blurred and short-sighted, even when we're pointed in the right direction. It is frightfully easy, after we've experienced some special answer to prayer or a personal victory, to relax and let our faith feed on that past experience. But to do that is to invite disappointment. There is no one experience, no one person or doctrine, on which we should pin the full weight of our believing. Our faith-focus must center on God alone.

If You See It You Can Have It!

I think focusing our faith on past experiences may be the reason we sometimes experience defeat in one part of our life after we've triumphed at some other level. Of course, past experiences can serve as reminders of God's goodness, but our faith-focus must be on God, not on something that happened in the past. Circumstances may change, as can our natural ability to cope, but *God does not change.*

At the same time we must be constantly aware that God's plan may be different from ours. For example, it is true that Jesus said, "All things are possible to him who believes" (Mark 9:23), but then we also read that those great Old Testament heroes and heroines "all died in faith, *not having received the promise"* (italics mine). There wasn't anything wrong with their faith, but God's eternal timing was different from theirs. Again, the focus of our faith must be on God and his timing.

Then, too, I'm sure you've heard people say, even as I have, that "God always answers prayer, but sometimes his answer is 'no.'" That's a clever rationale, but somehow I don't find it either helpful or satisfying. And when we're in trouble, it's a bit too cute. I think God's answer in such instances isn't "no"—but "something better." God wanted Adam and Eve to have "something better"—the whole garden, but all they were willing to see was some fruit on one tree. So often, in our near-sightedness, we are guilty of asking God for a "bauble" when he has something better, something real, for us.

So much of God's magnificent beauty can be enjoyed by a traveler in the Ozark mountains of Arkansas. Here we see an authentic display of the awesomeness and wonder of God's hand in creation. There's nothing gaudy or superficial about that vast panorama of majestic, tree-covered mountains, lush green meadows, and blue sky. To breathe in the clear mountain air and fill one's soul with the beauty of the landscape causes the sensitive person to share the mood of the ancient writer who urged his readers to "stop and consider the wondrous works of God" (Job 37:14) and to catch the mood of the psalmist who wrote, "The heavens are telling the glory of God, and the firmament proclaims his handiwork. Day after day pours forth speech, and night to night declares knowledge" (19:1-2).

But that same traveler, when stopping at one of the many gift shops that dot the highways, can also feast his or her eyes on the glitter of a carefully cut "Arkansas diamond." To the untrained eye it appears comparable to the finest New York's Fifth Avenue jewelers have to offer. But the $25.00 price tag advertises its artificial qualities. How easy it is to be taken in by the artificial or the second best when God has "something better" for us!

Another thing that can blur our faith-vision to where we are blinded to God's good possibilities for us is in the way we handle our past. I find that there is no surer way to become disheartened about God's present and future possibilities for me than to allow myself to become a prisoner of my past. Somehow it seems dreadfully easy for us to concentrate on our mistakes—on our self-inflicted wounds. And yet, to do this is to slam shut the door on a redemptive and faith-filled future.

Imprisoned by the Past

Dr. Martin Lloyd-Jones, noted English preacher and author, was asked to speak one evening with a man whose life seemed shrouded with defeat. Actually, Mr. Johnson was the local schoolmaster, but his influence was limited because of his dour and defeated attitude.

They weren't far into the conversation before Dr. Lloyd-Jones learned what it was that had so deeply scarred

If You See It You Can Have It!

the man's life. It seems that he had served on a submarine during World War I that had been torpedoed by the enemy. "Down we went to the bottom of the Mediterranean," he said, "and I've never been right since then."

Dr. Lloyd-Jones asked, "But what happened then?"

"Nothing," the man answered. "That's all there is to it."

To make sure he was hearing correctly, Dr. Lloyd-Jones asked him to repeat the story, and it ended exactly the same way, "Nothing. That's all there is to it."

"But what happened after that?"

"There's nothing more to be said," Mr. Johnson replied.

"Are you still at the bottom of the Mediterranean?" Dr. Lloyd-Jones asked. "No," the man replied. "We were saved by a rescue squad and then put aboard a hospital ship and returned to England."

Evidently, for the first time Mr. Johnson had been forced to tell the end of the story. Through all of the years he had been a prisoner of part of his past. But in this conversation Dr. Lloyd-Jones had broken the irrational barrier Mr. Johnson had put around himself. Now, he was no longer imprisoned "at the bottom of the Mediterranean." This experience opened up a whole new life for Mr. Johnson, and just a couple of years later he was ordained a clergyman in the Church of England where he served effectively for many years.

When Faith Interprets the Past

Faith has great power to interpret our past. We so often think of faith as a power that changes the future, but what it does to the past may be even more significant—getting our past in order gives the future a chance. This truth was wonderfully illustrated for me several years ago when I met a man whose life had been dramatically altered by an accident. The accident had been preventable, and he had every reason to harbor bitter feelings of resentment toward the person whose foolish mistake had caused it.

"After much prayer," my friend said, "I chose deliberately to see what good God might bring from the mess. And he has! There are benefits and blessings in my life that would never have been possible if it hadn't been for that ugly accident." He allowed faith in God to put the past in a proper perspective. Conditions hadn't changed, but my friend's faith enabled him to see those conditions in a new light.

Faith has certainly helped me to see the physical circumstances of my childhood in a new way. As seen through today's eyes, my childhood home was pretty grim. In my mind's eye I see a dimly lit living room that was very small and modestly furnished. A blanket served as our front door to keep out the cold in the winter time. In so many ways those depression years were dark and heavy.

But because of my faith I have happy memories of my childhood, and I'm filled with gratitude for my parents because of all they tried to do for us under the most difficult of circumstances. And I have warm feelings of appreciation for many of the people in our neighborhood and church who were interested in me. My faith has helped me to see how God used all of that in the shaping of my thoughts, ideas, and attitudes. Faith translates our past, interprets it, and gives it perspective.

But probably the thing that blurs and limits our vision beyond everything else is our low opinion of God. Our faith is weak because somehow we find it difficult to really accept the goodness of God. We talk about God's love and sing about it, but deep inside we evidently don't believe it because we don't act as if we do.

This is a strange phenomenon, and as I've reflected on it, two or three questions come to mind. Is our low opinion of God because so much of the preaching and teaching we've heard has made us fear God instead of believing the best about him? Did some of our early teaching lead us to see God as the Ultimate Policeman? Is it possible this childhood warning is responsible?—"Remember, God sees everything you do even if I don't."

Not long ago I saw a wall motto that gives us a marvelous response to questions like that. It read:

> GOD IS WATCHING YOU
> *He loves you so much, He can't take His eyes off you!*

I like that! There's nothing about God watching that should cripple us with fear or cause us to see him as the great Policeman in the sky who will get us if we don't watch out. The writer of Hebrews said it well when he wrote "that he [God] is the rewarder of those who diligently seek him." As sons and daughters of God, we can know that our heavenly Father wants the best for us—"see that, and you can have it."

Pursued by Grace

That's what the grace of God is all about! So often we think of God's grace only as the means of salvation. But that great "unmerited favor" of his pursues us all through life. John Newton, converted slave trader turned hymn writer, understood this well. Most of us remember him best for his "Amazing Grace" that tells of God's saving love. But he emphasized the ongoing grace of God in lesser known lines:

> Thou art coming to a King,
> Large petitions with thee bring,
> For His grace and power are such
> None can ever ask too much.

THE POWER OF BELIEVING

I remember reading about a seven- or eight-year-old slum boy who had lived in poverty all his life and was near starvation. When a social worker gave him a glass of milk, he asked, "How far down can I drink?" Consciously or unconsciously, most of us have something of that kind of an attitude toward God. When we hear or read about his goodness and mercy, we tend to place limits on it—"How much of this does he really want me to have?"

For me, at least, no one has ever pictured the grace of God better than Charles Wesley in one of his lesser known hymns. His language is almost playful, as if he was so elated with his newly discovered understanding of God's wonderful grace and goodness that he couldn't help breaking out in laughter. For someone who is hesitant or tentative in approaching God, Wesley's language might seem a bit audacious. But I'm inclined to feel that is only because we've for too long allowed ourselves to accept a negative idea of God. Here are Charles Wesley's delightful words,

> What shall I do to thank my God
> For all His mercy's store?
> I'll take the gifts He hath bestowed,
> And humbly ask for more.

There's an almost rollicking quality to Wesley's words. The most satisfying way I've found to explain his idea is to picture a boy who has just returned home from college or the armed forces. For his first meal his mother has loaded down the table with the foods that she knows he likes best. With great relish he polishes off the first plateful and then asks for a second helping. Is the mother offended by her son's appetite? Hardly! Nothing pleases her more than to see him enjoy what she has prepared for him. Maybe Charles Wesley had viewed just such a scene, for he had decided that

If You See It You Can Have It!

the only way we can properly thank God for his many blessings is to put them to good use in the business of our daily living and then say, "More, please."

It is possible, of course, to be presumptuous in our attitude toward God or to forget our responsibilities to him and take his grace for granted. But I have come to believe that the greater danger is in having such a low opinion of God that we underestimate his will for us and the confidence he has in us. The promise holds—God is the *rewarder* of everyone who tries passionately to live for him. God is not reluctant, nor niggardly, nor penurious! And yet, so often it is our low estimate of him—our lack of faith in him—that cripples us spiritually and robs us of the richness God intends for us.

With almost monotonous regularity books appear on the bestseller lists that urge us to dream big and give us step-by-step instructions on how to do it. And that's good as far as it goes. But our capacity to dream is so often limited to our own past experiences or to the experiences of others we trust. Most of these fail, though, to take into account our restless inner urge to focus our faith on a Power outside ourselves. Thus our dreams are limited to what *we* can see and feel.

Is Your Faith Too Small?

One of the most colorful characters in the Gospel story is the hardy Galilean fisherman, Simon, son of John. We don't know anything about his boyhood, but it is likely that he dreamed of being a great fisherman. When, as a boy, he played along the shores of that mighty inland lake, and listened to the tales of the fishermen while they mended their nets, he no doubt dreamed of the day when he would have a fishing boat of his own. He most surely fantasized hauling in a huge catch, dragging it to the shore, and then boasting about it in the marketplace. There is everything about the adult Simon we know to make us certain that his vision included being the best fisherman on the Sea of Galilee.

That was a good and worthy dream, but for Simon it was too small. It reflected the limited world in which he lived. In a way, it was like many of our dreams—a product of our environment and experience. And if this was all Simon was ever to see, it was all he would get.

But one day Simon met a new teacher along the shores of Galilee, Jesus of Nazareth. Jesus shocked Simon's dreams and said in effect, "So, you are Simon the son of John. From now on you will be called Peter"—the rock.

The Big Fisherman's new name would not only have surprised him, but it probably seemed inconceivable to his family and friends. After all, he was sort of an up-and-down fellow—a braggart who would swear his loyalty to you one day and then deny it the next. Anyone who knew him would have told you that it didn't mean much to get a piece of *that* rock!

But Jesus called him a rock and told him he would become a fisher of men. And eventually Simon became the most famous fisherman in all history. This is borne out by the fact that now, nineteen hundred years later, if we ask, "Who was the Big Fisherman?" someone is sure to answer, "Simon Peter."

Never in Simon's wildest dreams as a boy and young man would he have seen himself as a fisher of men, as a spokesman for Jesus' disciples, as the bold preacher to thousands on the Day of Pentecost fearlessly declaring "that God has made him both Lord and Christ, this Jesus whom you crucified" (Acts 2:36), and as the one who said to the crippled man at the gate called Beautiful, "I have no silver and gold, but I give you what I have; in the name of Jesus Christ of Nazareth, walk" (Acts 3:6). But it was this same Jesus Peter talked about who gave him a faith that enlarged his vision. There was nothing small now about Peter's dreams—they took in the world in which he lived as well as the world to come.

Faith to See Further

This is precisely why the apostle Paul prayed that the eyes of his reader's hearts would be opened and enlightened. And this is a prayer that we would do well to pray daily, for we need to see further than we do. Life slowly and steadily conditions our vision, teaching us what is possible or practical or "reasonable" to expect. But I also believe that we have a part to play, with the Lord's help, in the development of our vision.

People who are far more at home in God's great outdoors than I am tell me that an expert guide can find a path through rough terrain where a tenderfoot sees nothing but a mass of trees and tangled underbrush. That is because the guide has *developed* this skill by becoming sensitive to conditions that anyone could see if he or she was willing to invest time and concentration.

This reminds me of times when I've been out on one of the Great Lakes in a boat with an experienced pilot. Where I see nothing but rolling waters and waves, he knows how to read them and guide us safely to our destination. In all of this I see an analogy with our superficial attempts to meander through life concentrating on surface things. Because of a lack of vision, of faith, and our failure to perfect that faith-vision as best we can, we miss so many of life's richest and most rewarding experiences.

There is probably no folk-proverb more widely quoted than this one, "You never know what you can do until you try." These words are true whether it is said to a fourth grader who is struggling to excel in the high jump or to an entrepreneur who is planning to venture into a new business. But several years ago the popular psychologist and author Bonaro Overstreet gave that sentence a twist that is even more true, "You never try until you know what you can do."

The lesson we learn from this is that our attitude toward life is extremely important. For as Christians, we won't give God's power and our own ability a really honest chance until our eyes are opened to see the enormous possibilities that lie ahead.

Of Giants and Grasshoppers

After the historic Exodus-event the people of Israel worked their way across and up the Sinai peninsula to the southern border of Canaan. They set up camp and sent twelve spies on north to check things out. When the spies returned to camp, they all agreed that it was a rich and prosperous land. But ten of the spies gave a gloomy report. There was no way they could conquer those well-fortified cities and towns. And besides, alongside the "giants" who lived there, they looked like "grasshoppers."

Caleb and Joshua, the other two spies, saw exactly what their associates saw. Yet their eyes of faith saw themselves as overcomers. But the majority report won the day, and the Israelites turned back into the desolate Sinai desert. It wasn't until some forty years later that God permitted them, under Joshua's leadership, to begin their conquest of Jericho and Canaan. While before they had said, "We were like grasshoppers *in our own sight,*" now they moved boldly with eyes of faith to fulfill God's best for them. What was true then is true now. If we feel like a grasshopper in an impossible world of giants, we become one.

If You See It You Can Have It!

One of the most remarkable men I've ever known was Mr. A. W. Ziegelmann, a member of the first church I served as a pastor. He rang the church bell every Sunday morning, signalling the beginning of the service. With the little choir clustered nearby ready to sing the call to worship, A. W. would josh with all comers as he tolled out the Sunday morning welcome.

A. W. had a small business repairing lawn mowers and other outdoor equipment. But I hadn't been his pastor long before I learned that he was a blacksmith by trade and had worked at that job until he had a heart attack. He loved to tell about it—"The doctor said that I had no more than a year or two to live. But I said to him, 'Doc, I'll be one of the pallbearers at your funeral.' And I was! At the time I was stricken, though, I made up my mind that with God's help I was going to live." Then he would draw himself up to his full height and add, "And look at me now." He was a husky and powerful man. Here was a case in point, A. W. knew what he could do, so he tried.

It is this spirit, this vision, that was so much a part of our American way of life in the late nineteenth and early twentieth centuries. We were a nation full of hope, of faith, and nothing seemed impossible. Immigrants from Europe and Asia came to our shores expecting to find a better way of life. And they did.

Faith and the Future

In many ways it was kind of a crazy time, but our forebears had a vision of the future. They were convinced that nothing could stop them, and it didn't.

As head football coach at the University of Kentucky and the University of Alabama, Coach Bear Bryant became a legend in his own time. He was a great motivator of men, a great encourager. He didn't suffer many losses in his long career, but when he faced the possibility, he was frequently able to say or do something that would turn the tide.

On one particular day his team was being beaten badly when they went into the locker room at half time. They had been outplayed and were three touchdowns behind. It looked pretty hopeless. But Coach Bryant, with a ring of optimism in his voice, looked out at that bunch of dispirited and beaten young men and said in a booming voice, "Now, we've got those fellows right where we want them!" They caught his spirit, took on his faith, and went back to win the game in the second half.

There's an electric and contagious quality to encouragement. It inspires faith. One of the greatest encouragers of all times was the apostle Paul. In spite of the staggering difficulties that plagued the new young churches which he had founded and ministered to, his letters were always full of encouragement along with his sound teaching. One of his great qualities was that he saw these eager young Christians who were fresh out of paganism not as they were, but as they could be in Jesus Christ. In spite of their failures, he inspired them with words of encouragement.

There is just no way I can fulfill the debt I owe to my parents and teachers who became my encouragers as I tried out for the high school debate team and the a cappella choir. My parents faithfully attended even those events where I was only a minor performer. Still, their presence gave me confidence and faith in myself. I'm grateful for the forensics coach who said, "I think you're ready to represent Central at the next debate tournament, Ellsworth," and for the youth leader who said, "We'd like to have you speak for the youth program on the third Sunday of this month." Then, too, I remember those faithful friends who encouraged me when I felt the call to become a preacher. All of this great cloud of witnesses helped me to see what I couldn't fully see myself. They were God's instruments in opening my inner eyes and giving me a vision of what I could be.

I've come to believe that one of our noblest Christian tasks is in being "vision enablers"—encouragers. A man I know who has been especially used in a ministry to sick people says that he doesn't expect dramatic evidences of faith from those who are very ill. He says, "They need faith enough to ask for help, but beyond that, they have to lean on others. A sick person is already carrying a heavy load and needs supporting faith from the outside."

Then, too, I've known people who were undergoing severe emotional trauma. I remember one person who was in a state of deep depression saying, "I was so disturbed and depressed that I wasn't able to pray for myself. But I received strength in knowing that my friends were praying for me." By our support and faith we can help others to see, *so they can have.*

Let's Get Out of the Cellar

These closing years of the twentieth century are not times for "cellar living." Yes, there's a lot going on in our world that can sap the strength out of our faith and blur our vision. We live under the threat of nuclear war; the faces of starving people from Third World countries invade our living rooms by way of the television screen; the stock market is crazy at times; and innocent people are killed by terrorist bombs. It is terribly easy to become victims of despair.

Similar times prevailed in 1923 when Edmund Morel, a power in British politics, visited all of the European capitals. On his return to England he called on Prime Minister

THE POWER OF BELIEVING

Stanley Baldwin at Chequers to make his report. He had seen rags and poverty in Poland, hunger in Austria, and a likelihood of revolt in Hungary. He painted a dark and gloomy picture, and as he talked an oppressive black cloud seemed to descend on the two men.

Suddenly, Mr. Baldwin picked up a vase of brilliant red roses, and turning to his friend, he asked, "Do you like roses, Morel?"

"Like them—I love them," Morel responded. Shoving the vase into Morel's hand, Mr. Baldwin said, "Then, bury your face in this loveliness and thank God."

Mr. Baldwin knew that the beauty of the roses was as real as the threat of disaster then or in the future. Through eyes of faith his vision rose above the temporary sordidness and took in the marvelous glory of God at work in our world, so he could thank God!

Many years ago, Alistair MacLean, the great Scottish preacher, said this to his little highlands congregation one Sunday. "I read the fourteenth chapter of St. John's Gospel the other day, and as I did so, I saw my Lord's face shine through the printed page, and the world stood still."

That is the vision God intends for each of us to have. It is a faith-vision that focuses on God's life-changing, world-changing power. If we see it, we can have it. God wills it so.

Study Guide

Chapter 1.
1. In her pre-laughter days, Janis used the Beatitudes as an excuse for feeling bad. Can you recall instances where you yourself have used scripture or prayer as a "downer" to confirm your misery?
2. The author says that Sarah's faith-laughter was a mixture of belief and unbelief. Do you feel that God accepts such a mixture, or does He expect "pure faith"?
3. What part do you feel laughter has played in the survival of the Jewish people?
4. John Wesley said that a laugh is half a prayer. Is that true of any kind of laughter, or is there laughter that is not productive of goodness?
5. What instances have you known, in your circle of friends, where it seems that healing was aided by laughter and good cheer?

Chapter 2.
1. Is the author right in describing our attitude toward airplanes, elevators, etc., as "common faith," or is it just common sense?
2. The author says that some of the "greatest believers" he's ever known have simply put their faith in the wrong places. Think of someone in this category. How could their faith be turned toward the positive?
3. If God is the ultimate fact of our universe, what is "unrealistic" about trusting Him?
4. Most of us have known someone like the centurion, who— though not conventionally religious—seems to exercise strong faith. How do you explain such instances?

5. The author says he sees many cases of "faith-sickness"—that is, cases where people condition themselves to be ill. What circumstances in daily life have you observed which encouraged illness via despairing thoughts?

Chapter 3.
1. Is faith a fairer standard of judgment before God than good conduct? Why?
2. It was so irrational for Adam and Eve to believe the serpent rather than God. What instances have you seen where you and I do the same sort of thing?
3. The author says that conversion is a kind of return to Eden. How much of an Eden could we make of our personal lives if our faith were better directed? How much of a difference could we make in the world as a whole?
4. The author contends that many of us have a negative image of God in our minds. What are some of your negative images of God, and where did you get these ideas?

Chapter 4.
1. Can faith really play a part in daily business life, as Herbert Taylor seemed to feel? Have you known anyone who has practiced his faith that effectively, even if on a smaller scale?
2. Almost every great faith-hero, from Abraham to Albert Schweitzer, carried others with them in their enterprise. What right did they have to expect this kind of "second-hand faith" from other people?
3. Joni Eareckson Tada, Captain Scott and Robert Louis Stevenson demonstrated a faith that has held on with courage, though without getting their answer. If they had more faith, would their prayers have been answered?
4. If, as MacDonald said, "the principal part of faith is patience," is patience then the best proof that one has faith?

Chapter 5.
1. Could it be that Noah's great faith developed precisely because he lived in such evil times? That is, does the strongest faith develop under negative circumstances?
2. How can you deal with a friend or associate whose conversation tends to be negative or faith-destroying?

Study Guide

3. Why are our church services so often marked more by painful solemnity, rather than by joy?
4. Martin Luther had a sustaining phrase: "I am baptized." What verse or song works effectively for you?
5. Clearly enough, such faith heroes as Noah, Abraham and Moses were not perfect people. Does this mean that faith has nothing to do with conduct and character?

Chapter 6.
1. What do you think is the difference between secular optimism and Christian faith?
2. The Vazquez commitment to thousands of hours of practice sounds like a combination of faith and staith. What experiences in your own life have required you to show your faith by tough effort? Would you call what followed a "miracle of faith"?
3. The author says that faith can heal experiences from the past by putting them in different perspective. Think of some negative experience from your past and see how faith will help you to interpret it in a new light.
4. Think of church services you have attended recently: have they sent you home with a lift? If so, what factors encouraged and inspired you?
5. Simon Peter no doubt had small dreams regarding his personal potential. What dreams have you outgrown, by God's grace? Which of your self-images are still too small?
6. The author says that it is God's will for us to live more victoriously and to enjoy more of God's favor. If this is God's will, why aren't more of us living that way?

Dr. J. Ellsworth Kalas is senior minister at Church of the Saviour (United Methodist) in Cleveland Heights, Ohio. He travels extensively in the U.S. and abroad, and has worked with a variety of congregations from farmers to athletes (in Green Bay), as well as business and professional people. His previous books include *Honey in the Lion*, *Our First Song* and *Pilgrimage*. He recently received honorary doctorates (D.D.) from Asbury Seminary and Lawrence University. He is also one of the featured video lecturers in the *Disciple* adult education program sponsored by the United Methodist Church.